CW01431370

Contents

Publisher:

YSP - Your Scaling Partners Publishing

Action Media Solutions

2 Rue Benoit Oriol

42400 St Chamond

Printing Company: Amazon (Poland)

Price: 25 Euros

Dépot légal: 06/2025

DISCLAIMER

Purpose and Scope

This book is intended for *informational* and *educational* purposes only.

The content **does not** replace the necessity for *professional counsel* in finance or law or medicine or business matters.

The material appears exactly as written with no guarantees attached to any portion of it.

No Guarantees and Disclaimer of Liability

The author and publisher of this book make no representations or warranties of any form, whether expressed or implied, about the completeness, accuracy, suitability, reliability, or availability of the information, products, services, or related graphics contained within this book for any purpose.

Any reliance you place on such information is strictly at your own risk.

The author and publisher maintain no responsibility for damage from using this book and its included information because they disclaim all liabilities regarding *direct* or *indirect* or *incidental* or *consequential* and *special* or *exemplary* damages.

Individual results may vary. Your success depends on your efforts, dedication and prevailing market conditions.

Disclosure for affiliate links

Hey there, savvy reader!

Just a quick heads-up:

This book contains affiliate links.

What does that mean for you?

Purchasing through these links enables me to receive a small commission without affecting your purchase cost.

Consider this as your opportunity to endorse the author.

Anyhow, I only ever link to products that I think will be useful to you and that I think highly of myself.

Thanks for being awesome.

Income Claims and Metaphorical Language

Any income or earnings statements are *illustrative examples* only.
There are **no guarantees** of specific income or results.

AI Technology Risks and Ethics

AI technology is evolving fast.
Users need to understand both the ethical issues and the related duties which AI usage entails through responsible privacy protection as well as equal treatment of users and unbiased operation.
AI should thus be seen as a *complement*, rather than a *substitute* for human judgment and values.

Legal Considerations and Ethics

You remain accountable to follow all regulations and laws which exist in your local area.
Users must adopt ethical practices when employing AI tools as well as in their creation of AI-generated content.
Legal implications of using AI in your own jurisdiction should be known.

Intellectual Property and Data Protection

The correct attribution process together with proper licensing requirements needs to be observed for content generated with Artificial Intelligence tools.
You need to maintain original work and prevent any violation of intellectual property rights.
Make sure to safeguard your personal information together with your customer information during your usage of online AI tools.

Updates and Changes

The technology behind AI and the conditions of the market could change very fast.
Keep updated with the fresh development and updates.

Reader's Responsibility

You are responsible for how you apply the information in this book.
Seek professional advice when necessary.

Accuracy of Information

All effort has been made to present accurate, up-to-date, reliable, and complete information.
No warranties of any kind are expressed or implied.
Readers acknowledge that the author is not engaged in rendering professional advice.
The information in this book is derived from a variety of sources, accuracy and reliability of which might vary.
Reading this book implies your acceptance of this disclaimer which states that the material exists for educational purposes only and you take full responsibility for your application of the information. Seek professional counsel from experts before executing financial choices or applying guidance from this book.

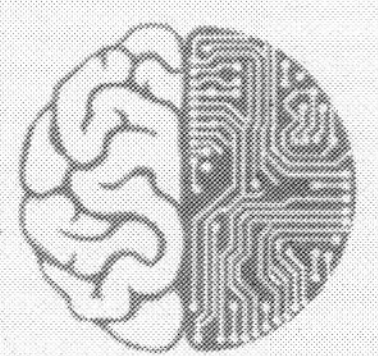

Introduction

⚠ Skip ahead, and no AI strategy will even matter.

WARNING

Look, we get it. Intros can be *snoozefests*. You are also thinking, 'AI, where is the AI?'. And you might be halfway through this thinking you must have opened a different book by mistake. The truth is, however, if you skip this intro, you're skipping the **cheat code** to the entire game.

Right then, Jung time.

Have you ever been exposed by any means to the name of **Carl Jung**? He clearly knew what he was talking about. He delivered this powerful truth:

"Man is not the master of his own fate; the subconscious holds the reins."

. . .

This statement is blunt, but it is also true. Most of the time, we act under a *false sense of conscious control*, while the **subconscious dictates** what we do.

William Wordsworth expressed a similar idea more gently:

"Your mind's a garden. Your thoughts are the seeds. You can grow flowers. Or you can grow weeds."

Wise words indeed from William. Our thoughts are powerful. *Your reality is what they build one flower at a time, or one weed at a time.*

Meet Mike.

It's morning. Yet, Mike appears as if he *wrestled a bear all night. And lost.* He's been up all night. *Chasing the online dream.*

Across the room, a woman laughed, her face lit by the Bali sunsets flashing on her laptop. Young, carefree, she practically vibrated with an *easy success*. She looked like... *Everything Mike wasn't*. She *believes in herself*. You can see it. You can tell by her posture, her energy, her being.

Mike watches—*envy twists his gut*. He knows the same strategies, uses the same tools. So *what gives? Why isn't he living large?*

Unbeknownst to Mike, her entire upbringing was shaped by people who saw the world as *full of opportunity*.. She was *told she could do anything*, she was *supported*, she was *encouraged*. She *never questioned if success was possible*—so she just moved like it was. She doesn't even know it, but *her thoughts are in line, her actions are easy*. She ***expects*** *that things will work out* and, somehow, so far, they have. She ***foresees things coming together*** **... and they do, for some reason.**

Mike, on the other hand, is **fighting his own mind. Doubt and fear** sit in the driver's seat, and no strategy can fix that. He's **stuck. Drowning in self-doubt**. **Nega-**

tive feedback loop. His inner monologue's a broken record of "what if I fail?"

Mike's problem isn't a **lack of knowledge**; it's a **lack of belief**. He's trapped by **negative thinking**. His **inner critic** runs the show. That inner voice? Broken record of fear and insecurity. He's his **own worst enemy**. He has forgotten that *the world reacts to the energy that we put out*.

The thing about some people is that they simply function at a different level. Take this woman. She's got a **cheat code hardwired in**, running on *pure, environment installed programming*. Oh, and to top it off she is *completely oblivious* to the massive advantage that this gives her. Ask her seriously where her *"natural" talent* comes from. She'll be as lost as Mike. Neither of them can really explain her seemingly *effortless success*.

Which is why **Joel Brown** nailed it—

"The only thing that stands between you and your dream is... The will to try. The belief that it is actually possible,"

Imagine. You find yourself in a tennis match preparing to battle against your *sworn opponent*. You've *lost a hundred times in your head*. Normally, you choke. **But today is different.** *You believe you can win. You know you've got this. Unshakeably confident. You're a different person. You play differently. You move differently.* That belief fuels you. Before you know it? You win. **Boom.**

So, Mike—**LOSE THE NEGATIVITY.**

Rewrite your internal script.

Believe in yourself—world has no choice but to catch up.

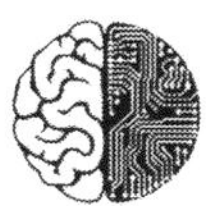

TRUTH BOMB (No Woo-Woo). *Just facts.*

Here's the deal.

Your subconscious? Dictates **99%** of your actions. It's a pre programmed script you are replaying over and over. Want different results?

Rewrite the script!

Want Proof?

Ever feel stuck? Like you're on autopilot? Same actions—same results? That's your **SUB CONSCIOUS**. Friend. *It's running the show.* **Time to grab the wheel.**

> ***Success starts in your head.*** *You absolutely must* ***BELIEVE*** *it before you see it. You need to* ***BELIEVE.*** *Before you can achieve.* ***Believe first, achieve second.***

Ready to upgrade your life? *Simpler than you think. Needs guts though—*

- Stop looking back. Past failures teach your brain failure. To create more of the same. **Forget about where you are at currently and look to the future you desire.** Imagine it vividly. Feel the positive vibes. Change your vibration.
- An aware person thinks ACTIVELY. They choose their thoughts *consciously*, regardless of what's going on around them.
- Set a **clear goal**. No destination means wandering. You'll just drift. Thanks to your outdated subconscious GPS. **Know where you're going.**
- Make a real **DECISION** to achieve it. Not *"I'll try."* Not *"Maybe."* **Decide you WILL achieve it.** Goals without decision are just wishes. **Burn the boats.** Commit **100%**. *Magic happens then.*
- Be **decisive**. Winners choose fast and stick. Unsuccessful people make them slowly and change course like the wind. The secret? **SELF-CONFIDENCE.**
- **Believe in yourself.** Even if it feels absurd. *Sometimes ignorance helps.* Less thinking—more believing. You know? *Stupid people achieve more often than not.* They don't overthink it. They **BELIEVE** with quadrillion percent of their being. Their brains find easy ways.
- **Believe it WILL be easy.** When you give your brain a good positive challenge, it will surprise you as to how resourceful you really are.
- **Banish Worry and Doubt**: Worry and doubt (often due to the unknown), when impressed on your subconscious, become anxiety itself. **Starve them out!**

You're in control. Change your thoughts? Change your life.

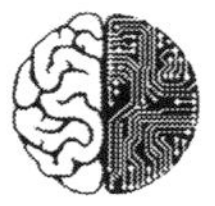

L*ife's a trip, right?*

- Financial stress? Keeps you up at night. *We've all been there.*

- Advice on money? Everyone's got it. Mostly confusing.
- Advice? Real? Practical? *Feels impossible to find.*
- Generic, complicated info? *Thanks, but no thanks.*

Deep down? You want a **clear path**. A **better life**. **Control over time**. **Control over money**. You need a **simple map**. **Real results**.

TIME FOR A MENTAL TUNE-UP. *SERIOUSLY.*

Remember **Carl Jung**? *That smart guy?* He also said:

> "Until you make the unconscious conscious, it will direct your life and you will call it fate."

Your subconscious is a **GPS**. Stuck on autopilot. Programmed by old beliefs. Bad habits. It drives you. Destination? Unknown. Or most likely—*more of your current reality*. More of the same.

Time to hack the system!

Think of it like this.

Your mind's **GPS** defaults to old routes.

Update it.

Input "success," delete "can't."

You keep hitting roadblocks? Dead Ends?

You need to do a **software update** for your internal **GPS**. The first thing you have to do is to find **outdated programming** – those negative thoughts that keep you from moving forward. Next, choose what you want your **dream destination** to be, and input those coordinates into the **subconscious**.

Note the order from Thought to Action and Belief.

1. **Trigger.** Something happens. A sight, a sound, a feeling.
2. **Think.** Your mind reacts. First impression.
3. **Choose.** See the good. OR focus on the bad. *Your choice.*
4. **Inner Shift.** This changes you inside. Light or heavy. *Your choice shapes it.*
5. **New Feeling.** Hopeful OR discouraged. You feel the difference.
6. **Decision Time.** Act on hope. OR react to fear. *The choice is yours.*
7. **Action.** Bold move OR hesitant step. *Your choice dictates your action.*
8. **Belief.** Confidence grows. OR doubt creeps in. *Your choices? Build your beliefs.*
9. **The Cycle Continues.** New trigger. New thought. Choose again.

Choose consciously. Your actions are built of what you think, which in turn build your reality.

UPGRADE PLAN—*EASY PEASY*:

- **Thoughts.** Trade *"I can't"* for *"I CAN!"* Replace *"Not good enough"* to *"I'm CAPABLE"*. Exchange *"What if I fail?"* with *"What if I SUCCEED?"* **Think upgrade.**
- **Feelings:** Positive fuel only—*hope, guts, excitement.* Fear's out.
- **Beliefs:** Positive thoughts on repeat? You'll believe 'em. Deep down. You **ARE** capable. Deserving. Worthy. **Believe it.**
- **Actions:** Rock-solid beliefs? Action's automatic. Internal GPS says, "*Confidence turn, then straight to success!*" **Let's go.**

Don't focus on now. Current problems? Trigger old negativity. **Fix your eyes on the goal.** See it. Feel it. Let it pull you forward.

Personally? I flat-out refuse to entertain negative thoughts or doubts. *IT'S A CHOICE.* I choose to interpret every outcome as positive.

I believe **ALL THINGS**—literally—**IN THE ENTIRE UNIVERSE**—work towards **MY** ultimate good. Secretly. Yes—*even challenges.*

This is **NOT** wishful thinking.

A proper understanding of the power of your **subconscious mindset** is required. Only then can you reprogram it. You absolutely have this power. **Let's put it to work.**

Still reading?

Good. Let's rewire that brain.

You've got this!

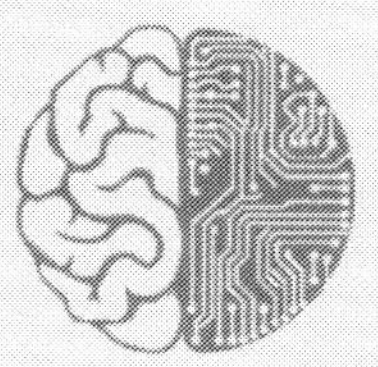

From WTF to Well-Formed Text

This Book Barely Survived Its Author.

Shocking Fact:

My editor considered early retirement because of my first draft.

Dear Time-Conscious Reader,

This is a *historical artifact*, the author's note I wrote when I believed "w/" was a correct substitute for "with." Imagine it as *ancient manuscript* with a caffeine stain in an old library, only the library was my laptop and ancient means 'last month.'

There is a time when I had a problem. A serious problem. My editor staged an intervention and I have gotten a new life as a changed man. A man who now spells words completely! This book is fixed—*editor victory*. But this note stays—*proof of my journey from chaos to words*.

Think of it as an inside peek glimpse into a writer's mind prior to intervention.

ORIGINAL NOTE—PURE CAFFEINE FURY:

Dear Reader. Let's talk coffee. And speed.

This book began fueled by coffee. Lots of coffee.

I have groundbreaking research. Mind-blowing insights. Ready for your brain.

My brain works fast. My fingers do not. My typing? Snail speed compared to thought speed.

So I took shortcuts. My editor called it a problem.

I called it efficiency. Developed over years. 3 AM texts. Late-night research.

Abbreviations became a habit. A bad one? Maybe.

My editor tried a cure. It failed.

Three keyboards died for this book.

Meditation seemed slow. Typing lessons dull. I chose chaos. Organized chaos.

You will find shortcuts here. Like 'w/' for "with". 'Info' for "information".

Why?

More ideas. Less paper.

Your brain? It actually processes abbreviated info faster. (science backs this up[1])

My keyboard thanks me

But don't worry... I am not yet full text speak on you. This is my experiment towards literary efficiency. Since Shakespeare invented new words I should be allowed to shorten words properly. Right?

Here is your guide. Your key to speed:

- & – and
- b/c – because
- btwn – between
- dev – development
- doc – document
- e.g. – example
- esp. – especially
- hrs – hours
- incl. – including
- info – information
- intro – introduction
- kinda – kind of
- max – maximum
- mins – minutes
- prev. – previous
- stat – statistic
- tech – technology
- v. – versus
- w/ – with
- w/o – without
- wanna – want to

These abbreviations should be thought of as *mental shortcuts*. These will be processed by your brain the same way it automatically processes "Dr." as "Doctor" within minutes.

Let's go,

Tigran

[1]Not actual science. But it felt true. Right?

P.S. My editor tried their best. They're now in therapy too. Seriously.

P.P.S. If you skip this page and later complain about abbreviations, my editor will personally send you a ***strongly worded letter***. In long-form.

Post-Rehabilitation Update:

Three editors, two therapists, one typing coach later? This book? Fully rehabbed. *Fully rehabilitated* into proper English. Abbreviations were lovingly expanded. All of them. Coffee addiction? Still here. Stronger than ever.

My editor reports successful therapy completion. Doing great. Thanks for asking. And they really want me to mention this book is ***100% abbreviation-free.*** They are unreasonably proud of this fact. It's cute, honestly.

I have newfound respect for English. And slower fingers.

Tigran

P.P.S. If you somehow make it to an abbreviation I did not record, my editor will send you a cookie. And an apology.

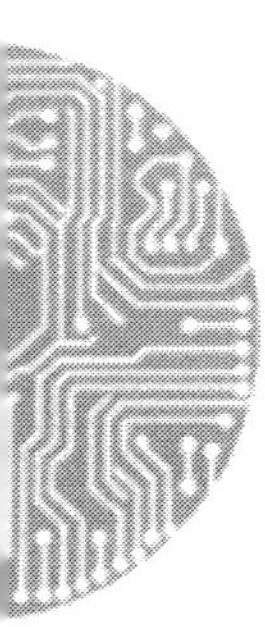
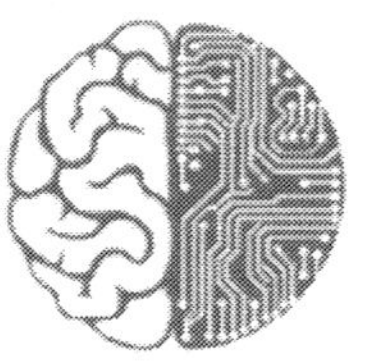

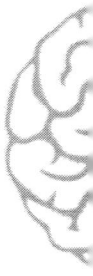

⚠ ESSENTIAL FIRST STEP

Discover Your Personalized AI Income Path

CRITICAL NOTE: In order to get the most out of this book, you first need to know your ***ideal AI income path*** by taking the quiz below. This assessment will directly inform how you apply the strategies in this book series to your situation.

Why This Matters:

- ***A Personalized Course:*** You'll be given a course that supports and complements this book.
- ***Clarity.*** Without clarity you are likely to spend valuable time in the wrong strategies that do not match up with your strengths or interests.
- ***Focus.*** The results will be your *North Star* throughout this book and the whole series.

How to Get Started:

- ***Digital readers—Start Here.***
- ***For Print Readers visit:* go.yspweb.com/AI-income-quiz**

Be sure to type the entirety of it out including "https://".

Do not want to type that long web address? No problem! Notice the unique striped pattern in the shape of a square? Below? That's a *QR* – a *QR code,* that is – a digital shortcut. Here's all you need to do:

1. Grab your smartphone
2. Open your camera

3. Point it at the square. Don't take a picture.
4. Tap the link that pops up. Boom.

Nothing happened? Your phone might be shy. It may need a QR reader app. Search "***QR code reader***" in your app store—*Google Play* or *Apple App Store*. Install a free one. Then, try scanning the code again using the app.

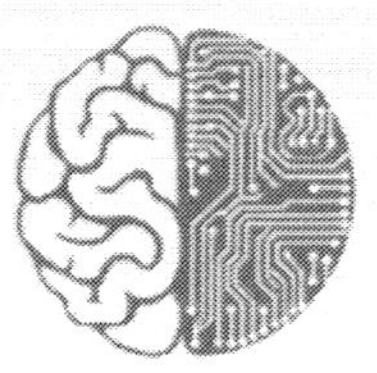

The Promise of This First in a 3 in 1 Book

This *"Book I"* is your invitation to the first 4 days of a 21 day challenge. It's also the first of a 3 in 1 series. The goal of the series? Will help you build your perhaps very first online passive income stream. And the best part? ***AI***. No fluff. No outdated theories. Just strategies that work. Straight-to-the-point. ***AI powered.***

The goal of this *Book I*?

Become an AI Whisperer. No, really. We'll break down AI. Like it's a Lego set. Even if you're starting out. We'll be bullying our **AI slave robots** at each and every step of the way. No mercy.

We want ***SMART*** work, yes. Working hard is neither goal nor necessary for success. We WILL DELEGATE most of the HARD work to our AI underlings.

That being said...

This Series is a ***Tool***, no Magic Lamp (but very close).

Look, I need to be upfront. If you simply sit there, you won't get rich overnight. Anyone who promises that is selling snake oil. But you need to put in the absolute minimum required to set up **systems of leverage**.

You need to move the needle. By picking up the tools. By taking action towards your goals other than passive learning.

Think of it like this. We are giving you state of the art kitchen equipped with all the gadgets and the ingredients. We'll teach you the recipes. But you gotta do the cooking. We will also be sharing exclusive bonuses and resources with the newsletter's subscribers to ensure that you have every ingredient needed to succeed. It should be viewed as your secret stash of gourmet ingredients.

This is a ***Partnership***. You? ***The Boss***, Us? Your Advisory team. Your success is ultimately built by ***YOUR*** hands. Our ***SOLE*** mission is to provide the best damn blueprint we understand will help you achieve success.

A Bit About Me

It shall be known as confessions of a recovering shiny object chaser.

Have you ever attempted to chase the next big business scheme?

Yeah, me too.

I've been in the trenches. My resume reads like a business model buffet. The list is long—*dropshipping—Amazon FBA—digital products—SaaS*. You name it—I tried it. The whole shebang... All over the map.

I also have a past life "9 to 5" background in *IT Consulting* and later *Sales* (yeah, cold calling was part of the deal), not to mention operating an *Amazon FBA* store on the side and later running a successful service based marketing agency (*Facebook Ads SMMA*).

Mixed bag? Understatement.

Then **AI** showed up. **AI Automation**. The **Consulting Agency Space**. The rest? Still writing that chapter.

The ironic thing here is that those other business models work. They really do. The secret isn't the model. It's this—***not quitting***. The ones who succeed are just stubborn. They stick around. They become experts. Hard times come, but they do not break; they become better.

Shiny object syndrome? Real. I feel you.

The temptation to chase the *get rich quick* dream is there. I tried my fair share. Some attempts were better than others.

Take it from me.

AI isn't just another fad.

It's here to stay.

It will revolutionize business.

It will revolutionize life itself.

Consider it your ticket.

Unprecedented freedom.

Unprecedented success.

Best time ever to be an entrepreneur—especially as a solo player.

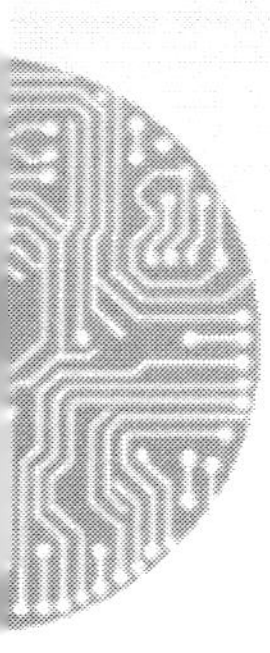
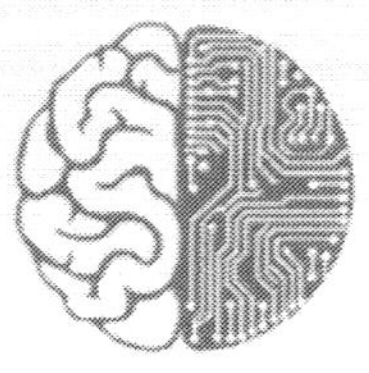

How to Use This Book

This series is organized as **21 days of challenge**.

Daily bites prevent brain indigestion.

The days consist of a mix of *theoretical insight* and *practical exercises*. My advice? Take it slow and steady. Think marathon, not sprint. One day at a time. Absorb the concept. Then do the exercises right away. This works. You learn better by doing.

To make your journey smoother, you get a **Prompt Book** alongside the theoretical content. **Download your digital PDF copy (https://go.yspweb.com/Prompt Book1)** and use two devices (tablet and computer) or a split-screen setup.

This way, you can easily see the **Prompt Book** while you read. Plus, digital means easy copying and pasting of prompts and templates. No re-typing. Or printing headaches.

The book is divided into two sections: a theoretical part and a practical workbook. Both are important, sure. But the exercises in the workbook? That's where things click.

Instead of reading all the theory first, I strongly urge you to complete the **Day 1** exercises in the workbook immediately after finishing the **Day 1** theory. Then, move on to **Day 2** theory and its corresponding exercises, and so on. This is critical because the concepts build upon each other. Skip **Day 1** exercises and try to jump into **Day 2** theory? You'll be lost. Each brick needs to be laid in its proper place for the structure to be sound.

Set Yourself Up

For the best shot, use a laptop or PC. Two windows side-by-side—ideas on one side—workbook on the other. Browser? Duplicate the tab or add a third window for your AI assistant. For copying and pasting of prompts.

Trust the process.

. . .

Ready to Take Action?

This is the point of it.

Have you heard the story about the bookworm who read everything he could about swimming but drowned on his first dip into the water?

Don't be that bookworm.

You can devour every self – help book there is, but words without action are just words stacking in your head. This is not the "just in case" type of learning to prepare for some future exam. This is "just-in-time" learning. You learn it, you do it. Right now.

Analysis paralysis? More like analysis paralyzed! Instead of being overwhelmed by research and self-doubt we have chosen to implement the *"iterative approach."* Test it out. See what happens. Try again. But this time better.

Ready to hit the gas?

Download the free **Prompt Book PDF**. Your co-pilot for this ride. Keep it open right next to the main book.

If you're reading off the print version here is the link (make sure to type out the https://):

`go.yspweb.com/PromptBook1`

Or scan this QR code:

. . .

That being said, having the promptbook on your phone defeats the entire purpose. Facilitating copying and pasting of prompts. What you can do instead is scan and download the pdf on your phone and then maybe send it to yourself via email.

21 days.
That's all it takes.
Challenge yourself.
Get a little uncomfortable.
Let's go!

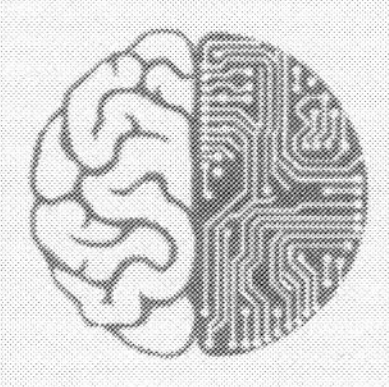

Bookmark this web page: Your Up-To-Date AI Tool Finder

Curated. Categorized. Continuously Updated.

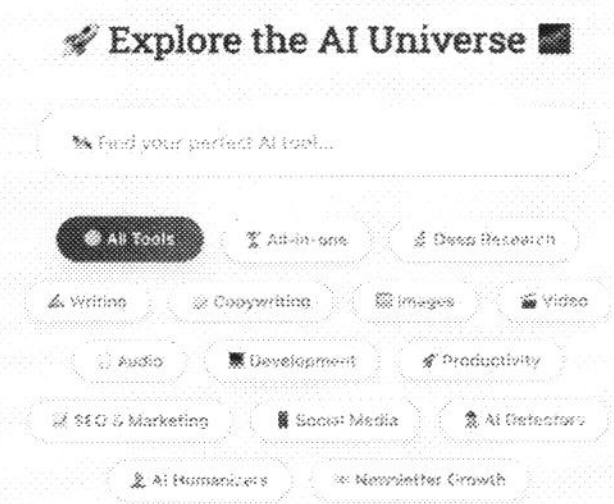

Interactive tool grid. Filter by category. Find exactly what you need! (The mobile browser version may not support all tools and comparison features.)

👉 To access visit: **`yspweb.com/tools`**

Or scan this QR code 👇

SP
PUBLISHING
TIGRAN G. VOSKANYAN

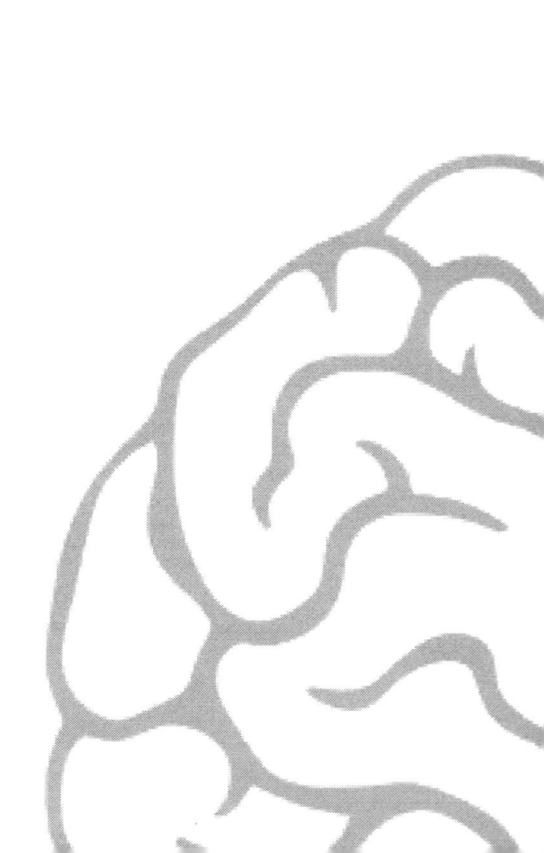

Book I

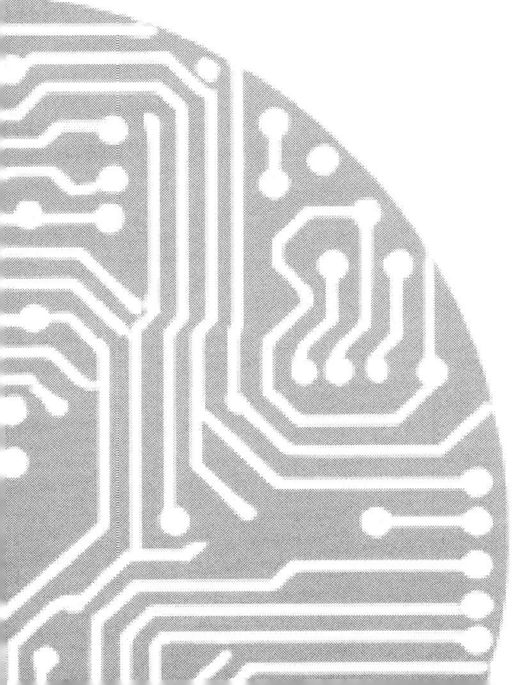

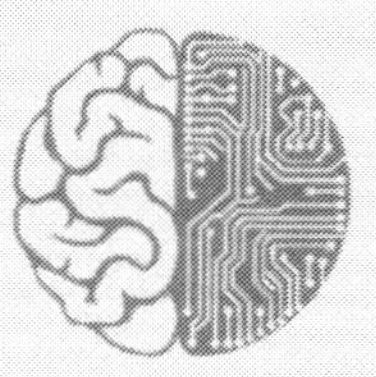

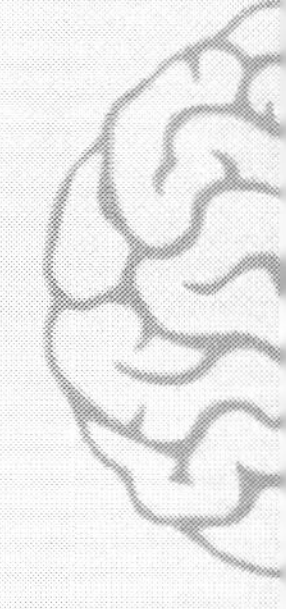

Day 1

YOUR BRAIN. NOW AI.

3 AM. Laptop glow. Blurry eyes. Mysterious wrist cramps. Backache. Caffeine crash. Sound familiar?

You want the online money secret. Everyone does.

The secret isn't secret. It's **AI**.

Alvin Toffler nailed it years ago.

"The illiterate of the 21st century will not be those who cannot read and write, but those who cannot learn, unlearn, and relearn."

This is your **AI crash course**. Pay attention. Freedom might follow.

Remember dial-up? Waiting years for a picture? AI moves faster. *Much* faster. Things get interesting now.

The AI Advantage:

The market's exploding. *$93.5 billion in 2021*. Nears a trillion by 2028. That's serious cash.

The global amount added by AI by 2030 could be *$15.7 trillion*. Maybe buy some AI stock? Or learn to use it?

Businesses agree. *83% of them*. They aren't wrong.

AI: Your Crash Course

First, the basics:

- **Machine Learning** can be understood through comparing it to the process of teaching new skills to pets. Rather than use words, you use data. Lots and lots of data. The data is something that the machine learns and becomes better off over time.

- **Deep Learning**. Imagine machine learning. On steroids. And it uses powerful 'neural networks' to analyse massive amount of data.
- **Natural Language Processing**. NLP. Can you recall when you went back and forth with your phone's voice assistant? Those conversations (sometimes) are made possible by NLP. NLP lets computers grasp human language.
- **Cloud Computing**. No, not that kind of cloud. Access AI tools online. No need for a home supercomputer. Think renting a Ferrari instead of welding one together. Way easier.

AI. Your New Best Friend. For Profits.

What is AI? Machines doing human things. Learning. Problem-solving. Making decisions.

They use data. Find patterns. Predict outcomes. Powerful stuff.

AI's Three Flavors: Narrow, General, Super

- **Narrow AI (ANI):** This is the specialist. Good at one thing. Your narrow AI buddies would be Siri, Google Assistant, Alexa.
- **General AI (AGI)**—The target. Human thinking inside metal. Still cooking.
- **Super AI:** Smarter than us. Let's hope it's friendly. For now, it's just sci-fi.

Where We Sit

Forget AGI and ASI for making money today. The AI that matters today is **Narrow AI**.

Narrow AI. Small Tasks. Big Wins.

- **What they do.** Voice recognition. Translation. Data crunching...
- **Why we like them.** They do the boring stuff. We get things done.
- **Current State.** Beats us at spam fighting, facial recognition, recommendations and so on. However, it can't think outside its box.

General AI. The Future is...Uncertain?

- **The Goal.** Machines that think like us. Or better.
- **The Reality.** Not there yet. Building a brain is hard.
- **The Debate.** Will it happen soon? Will it take over? Nobody knows!
- **Current State.** Still a dream. Scientists have not yet succeeded in decoding the human brain.

Predictions:

- Elon Musk: Thinks AGI arrives by 2029. Big claims, big brain.
- Others disagree—Human intelligence is a tough nut.
- Recent AGI buzz is always flying around.
- OpenAI's Q*. It has reportedly been found to be able to do math. Don't get too excited. It's basic stuff.
- AGI in Your Pocket. Imagine AGI in your phone. Near, but still some distance away.
- The Claude language model by Anthropic: This one's a bit spooky. It might be self-aware. It might have agency. Time to panic? Maybe not. But definitely interesting.

Speaking of Agents...

As the brain behind Google Brain, Andrew Ng stated that something was **BIG** in AI. Remember that time?

This is that time. He's hyped about **AI agents**. Imagine them as a new type of AI robot team, that is about to revolutionize AI this year. Forget fancy models. This is where the action is.

What Makes an AI "Agentic"?

Picture a smart robot squad. Each bot can:

- Act independently
- Make decisions
- Collaborate

Why Agentic Workflows Rock

These robot teams. Cool. But not only that. They're changing the game.

- Learn constantly: They improve.
- Adaptable. Curveballs? They'll improvise.
- Specializes like Olympic athletes
- Efficiency Boost. They are faster and more effective together.

The AGI Connection. Why This Matters.

Agentic AI? Our stepping stone. To AGI. Machines as smart as humans.

Here's how:

- Team Players—Copy human teamwork for goals.
- Complementary Strengths: Each bot fills in the gaps in the other's abilities.
- Step-by-Step Problem Solving. Complex tasks? They break them down.
- They act as Collective Intelligence, they learn from each other and they get smarter as such.
- They are Power in Numbers, that is, they take down challenges too big for a single bot.

Meet the Agentic A-Team

Here are the big names. And what they're doing.

- OpenAI is developing humanlike text understanding and generation models.
- Anthropic—Develops Claude—AI that thinks.
- Microsoft's Copilot: Office's new overachieving intern
- Meta (Facebook). Sharing the AI wealth. With open-source models. Like LLaMA.
- Google. Trying to build the language understanding and tasks automation AI.
- CrewAI: Builds user-friendly systems for creating AI agent teams.
- AutoGen is your tools for building custom AI agents however you wish.

Super AI. DON'T PANIC. It's Just a Theory

Super AI, or the super brainiac, is something humans are utterly not on par with. According to some, it is a long way off (if ever).

Where We Are Now:

• Narrow AI is king. Powerful. Ready. Essential for passive income.
• General AI is on the horizon. Exciting. Not prime time yet.
• Super AI is science fiction. Sleep easy.

Or in other words:

Narrow AI: One task. Like Siri.
General AI: Many tasks. Like us.
Super AI: Smarter than us. Not yet.

Your big takeaway for today? Right now you have narrow AI as a friend. Learn it. Use it. Profit from it.

The bottom line? AI isn't science fiction. Not anymore. It's here. it's powerful. And it's changing the world. Now is the time to become an apprentice and speak its dialect. We'll go into some of that later, but that's "prompt engineering".

For now? We'll look at the toolscape.

AI TOOLS

WARNING: ***This Chapter May Contain (Slightly) Expired Information!***

Well, you are about to meet some of the available AI tools. Awesome! However, this printed list is like a flip phone in a smartphone world.

Trying to become familiar with AI tools without being able to click and read through it is like high fiving on Zoom. Awkward, right?

For the very living, breathing, up to date version of this list along with links you can click on, see:

yspweb.com/tools

or
Scan this QR code 👇 (Picture of QR code should be here)

All-in-One Champs

- **Galaxy AI** (Netflix of AI models) Access all top models. One subscription.
- **Monica**: Integrates top AI Models for 1-click chat, search, writing, coding, image-generation and more for the price of one.

Writing

- Claude, OpenAI, Gemini: State of the art language models that generate text, image, sound and video (OpenAI SORA), answer questions, tackle creative tasks.
- **Rytr**: High-volume content. You set specific use cases, tones, keywords.
- **Writesonic**: Competitor of Rytr's.
- **Jasper AI**: Another competitor. High-volume content. With templates.
- **Copy.ai**: Persuasive marketing and sales copy focused competitor.

Images

- **Artistly**—Cheap all-in-one art maker—editor.
- **Phot AI**. Photo editing and image generation tools that are based on AI.
- **Fluxai**. An AI image and art creation platform.
- **artsmart ai**: Focuses on creative and artistic AI image generation.
- **getimg.ai**: Suite for image generation, editing, enhancing.
- Stable Diffusion: Open-source image generation from text. Flexible, customizable.
- **Leonardo**—Full stack image generation.
- DALL-E: Unique image generation from text descriptions.

- MidJourney: AI design. Logos, branding. Photorealistic.
- **NightCafe**: Offers AI art generation plus a community aspect.
- Canva: Simple graphic design. Templates.

Video

Creating videos from text, tutorials, marketing clips.

- **Vsub**: Quickly create faceless videos using AI.
- **Zebracat**: Designed for creating impactful videos quickly.
- **Simplified**: Does social media management and text-to-video (and other things).
- **invideo AI**: Text in, video out.
- **KLING AI**. Powerful text to video generator courtesy of China.
- **Synthesia** (AI avatars for videos)
- **Lumen5**: Converts text to video.
- **Pictory** (Short videos from long content)

Audio

Voice generation, music, editing, transcription.

- **ElevenLabs** (Scarily realistic speech)
- Suno.ai (AI music from text!)
- Descript (Edit audio/video by editing text)
- AIVA: Handles AI music composition.
- Sonix: Audio and video transcription.

Development

- GitHub Copilot. AI coding assistant.
- Hugging Face—Platform for open AI models.
- TensorFlow. Open-source platform.
- PyTorch. Open-source ML library.

Productivity

- **Make** (App automation)
- **Zapier** (More app automation)
- **Flowlu**: Projects to internal processes, manage it all in one affordable software.
- **Notion AI** (AI notes, tasks)
- monday.com: Collaborative project management.

SEO and Marketing

- seoClarity. Keyword research. Optimization. Analytics.
- Ahrefs. Backlink analysis. Keyword research.
- Moz. SEO audits. Rank tracking.

Social Media Management

- **Simplified**: Social Media Management + text to anything platform
- **Pallyy**: Social media scheduling.
- Hootsuite. Scheduling. Monitoring. Analytics.
- Buffer. Social media scheduling.

Email Growth

- **SparkLoop**. Growing your newsletter list.

AI Content Detectors

- **Winston**
- **GPTZero**
- **Originality**

AI Humanizers (Human-like AI Content Creation and Paraphrasing)

- **Writehuman**
- **Stealthwriter**
- **Undetectable**
- **gptinf.com**

Okay. You can talk AI now. Won't look totally lost.

Good for you!

But hold on.

Elephant in the room—AI is a wild stallion. Powerful—yes. But can knock you off. Hard. If you handle it wrong. Tomorrow? I'll show you how to avoid the pitfalls like a pro and will cover what they are in the first place. In other words, imagine learning to tame the beast before the beast throws you.

Day 1's in the bag—nice work! Now, hit those activities on the next page. No skipping! You need this stuff.

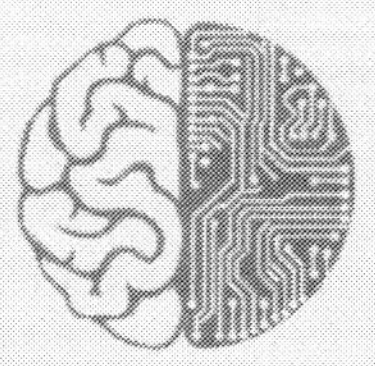

Day 1 Workbook

The Playground

Afraid of AI? Or just afraid of money? ***Let's fix both.***

Fear it away—AI isn't stealing your job today, but if you ignore it may.

Let's simplify APIs.

It is easier to imagine an API as a super efficient translator. It accepts what one application says, figures out what the other application should hear, and makes that conversation happen at a speed the user can trust and is secure. App A wants something? From App B? The API handles the introduction, the request, and brings back the goods. Simple as that. This translator just lets apps chat securely.

Why Start Your Journey Here?

Great question. The reason is that this is where you get your hands dirty—luckily, without even writing a single line of code.

Just when you signed up, OpenAI used to simply give away free credits. Either way, playing here is dirt cheap for learning.

More importantly? Lots of tools link to OpenAI's API. Consider it boot camp.

Experiment Time

OpenAI Playground is basically a sandbox. It is a user friendly place to chat with their models.

Here's the battle plan:

Just navigate to the OpenAI Playground.

Find it at: https://platform.openai.com/playground/

There will be options for different AI models. At this point you should avoid focusing on technical model names—trust me, no need to worry about them right now. Simply choose the latest, greatest one available. The 'System instructions' box remains empty for now. We'll get to that later.

See that main chat area? That's where you type. This is your prompt. Go on, ask it something. Whatever sparks your interest, tell it to write a poem, explain a concept, draft an email, play an instrument, create art, exercise, think, or whatever you want.

QUICK UPDATE

It is possible that I might really stop recommending openai.

They used to offer free credits for first time subscribers. I'm told they don't now. Needs confirming.

I have also personally lost a few hundred dollars worth of credits which I had bought because they expired and I don't believe having been notified :) Ouch. They expired. Poof. A heads-up would have been polite.

The funny thing is? It's not even THAT important with regards to the first exercise, which literally any assistant would do the job. Later in this book, you find better tools anyway.

Think of it this way:

ChatGPT is a set menu. Simple. Limited choices.

The Playground is kitchen access. Same ingredients. More control.

Quick Playground Perks:

- No Annoying Message Caps: Unlike ChatGPT sometimes.
- Usually cheaper than a ChatGPT subscription with its pay as you go structure
- Free credits to start (unless they discontinued)

Getting Started:

1. Click the link
2. Create a free OpenAI account
3. Check the Billing section—left side. See if credits appeared.
4. Find the Assistants tab. It looks like a little robot.
5. Create an assistant by filling out the system instructions (leave it blank for now) and choosing your desired model—keep in mind that any model would work for the day 1 exercise (the how to on the parameters is discussed on day 3 of the book but we'll get to that later)
6. Start chatting just like on chatgpt by writing your prompts in the thread section. It keeps the chat history.

Look, I still lean on the Playground for direct API access and building complex AI agents for myself and clients. It has its place.

But for everything else later in the book you'll discover Galaxy, Monica and other platforms.

They offer multiple AI models—different companies—one subscription. Better value. More options. You can also chat with some basic models for free.

Mission 1: Fish, Don't Follow

Forget step-by-step instructions. ***We're teaching you to fish.***

Your first task:

Go into the Playground assistant you just set up. In the Playground, type: "How do I create an OpenAI API key?"

Hit "Submit". Boom. The AI tells you precisely how.

See? You used AI. You have learned to tap into its power. This starts it all. Get ready for advanced tools. Enjoy this first taste.

Why would I create a key if I'm not using it currently?

Good question.

The API key is a backstage pass. The Playground is the audience view. Want your own show? Your own rules? Build something cool? You need the API key. It lets you use OpenAI models from other tools. Other platforms. Freedom.

Mission 2: Vision Quest for a Millionaire Mindset

Dive deep. Challenge money beliefs. Those limiting thoughts? **Smash 'em.**

Let's get real. Let's get rich. Let's get AI on this.

This is a Vision Quest. Less peyote. More playground.

Here's your toolkit:

- *OpenAI Playground.*
- Your Imagination. Free. Powerful. Ready.

Ready? Game on.

Step 1.

What's holding you back?

Write down THREE "What if" statements that expose your money anxieties. Be brutally honest.

The Example: 'What if I am not smart enough to earn money online? (Spoiler: You are.)

Example: "Perhaps I'm just not meant to be online business material (Spoiler: You clearly are.)."

Step 2. Flip it.

Take each fear to the Playground. For each fear-based "What if". Paste your statement.

Then, give OpenAI this instruction: Rewrite this statement from the positive and power perspective of someone who is already wealthy and successful.

Watch. OpenAI turns the script and demonstrates to you the power of positive 'what ifs'.

Step 3.

Feeling inspired? Good. Start a story with: "In my abundant future, I am..." Hit enter. Let OpenAI write the next sentence. Read it. Add YOUR next sentence. Bounce back and forth for 5-10 sentences. Dream big.

Step 4: Make Your Vision Visual

The sentence that oozes millionaire energy?

Use that sentence as a prompt. Feed that into an image tool (See Tools Section).

See your future in pixels. Keep that vision close.

What's Next? Day 2 Awaits!

Keep that AI vision handy. Flip to the Day 2 Theory section and keep the momentum going. Got questions? The Playground's got answers. Let's roll!

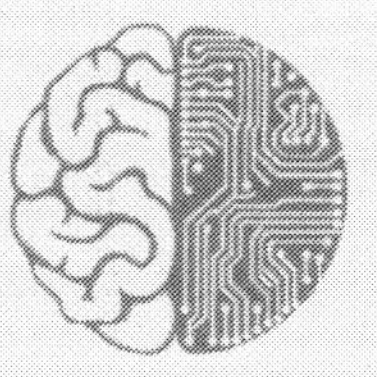

Day 2

THEY LIED TO YOU ABOUT AI

Privacy

Do you recall that incident of when you accidentally posted your whole browsing history on Facebook? With AI now? That mishap would be a walk in the park by comparison.

Yesterday? We explored AI's potential. Today, the topic at hand is about how AI is able to eat your privacy for breakfast.

AI finds value in every detail of your personal information.

AI loves your data. All of it. Your medical records—yep. Every embarrassing like? Oh yes. Handy? Sure. Creepy? If you like secrets? Absolutely.

How to Avoid Becoming an AI Buffet

- Read the fine print. Check the data collection details and distribution information of every app before installation. It is a digital prenuptial agreement.
- Choose companies carefully. Select those that regard your digital soul with respect. Avoid the highest bidder types.
- Share less. Consider privacy first tools. And remember: less is more (as it is when it comes to privacy).

AI is here to stay. **Protect your data**. *Stay aware*. **Be proactive**. The other option is to live as a digital recluse. Your choice.

CENSORSHIP

What would be this world with only one publisher? This publisher chooses the stories. It decides what you can read. Dangerous ideas vanish. This is the potential danger of closed AI. Big Tech? Controls these systems. The AI can be censored. Profit and politics might be their guide, not truth. Scary, right?

The way to fight for free speech is...

- Support open-source AI. Anyone can check and change the code. Big Tech loses power and it is transferred to the people. Censorship is hard.
- Demand Big Tech come clean. What criteria do they use to determine which statements an AI system can deliver? We need clear answers. Independent audits? Can ensure fairness.
- Welcome debate. A free society needs all views. Even uncomfortable ones. Let us judge the ideas on the basis of merit and not on fears.

The power of AI needs to exist for human benefit rather than be used as an authoritarian tool. Open-source and transparency? Key. AI should be made a tool of free speech, not censorship.

Closed Source

"I'm sorry, Dave. I'm afraid I can't do that."

HAL 9000's words send shivers. Through HAL 9000 we receive warnings about advanced artificial intelligence that eludes our understanding. We ought to discuss AI that is visible and AI that isn't.

Closed Source: The Black Box

Closed source is a locked vault. A black box. You can't see the code. You can't see the data. You have zero clue how it reaches its conclusions. It's like a shadowy company. Hard to trust. Who runs it? What do they want? We're in the dark.

Open source throws the doors open.

Open source

Open source is different. Open-source AI is an open book. Everyone sees the code. They can poke at it. They can share it. This builds trust. We understand how it works. We can fix problems. Like bias. It is a team project for better AI.

Why Open Source Matters:

- Accountability, for one. When the code's public, creators have nowhere to hide. Ethics suddenly become very visible.
- Open source is also an innovation because it's a global brain storming session. It is everyone's contribution that makes progress faster.
- Open-source: Since it is open, AI is democratized such that it is available to everyone. *Power to the people!*

No one, to be exact, ever said,

"I, for one, welcome our new robot overlords."

The AI revolution has arrived so the important question is not about our control of it but who has taken control.

BIAS IN NLP: AI'S GOT SOME PREJUDICE

AI's been called "the world's most talented parrot."

Ever been unfairly judged? AI knows the feeling.

That open source AI can punch back at the technology companies is something that we love. But even AI has flaws. It can be filled with biases just as we are. Some times, we are not even aware of this happening.

AI's Got Talent...Or Does It?

Suppose an AI is evaluating a contest that features music. Classical is its thing, but it falls asleep to punk rock. Why? It was probably trained on Mozart, not the Sex Pistols. It was trained on classical, not punk.

And AI job recruiters? Don't get me started. They can accidentally filter out entire groups of qualified people just because of biases hidden in the data they were fed. Talk about a bad hire!

AI's Biggest Blunders:

- Remember the *COMPAS* system? It was supposed to predict recidivism risk —whether someone might commit another crime. Sounds helpful, right? Except it was allegedly biased against Black defendants. **Not cool, COMPAS.**
- Or *Google Translate's* early pronoun problem? Google Translate: Assumed CEOs were "he" and nurses were "she"? It allegedly kept defaulting to "he" even when it made no sense.
- Train an AI on cityscapes and it could misidentify a deer as a particularly strange form of dog. It yields a few hilarious (and worrying) misinterpretations due to the limited data available.

HALLUCINATIONS

A lawyer ate penalties trusting AI's fake legal cases. Landed in court for citing fake cases. Big mistake.

We also want to discuss why you should soulcheck AI when you receive the answer.

AI Has a Wild Imagination. And not always in a Good Way.

AI is utterly creepy at mimicking human writing. But sometimes, it confidently states complete falsehoods. These AI lies are called "hallucinations."

AI Hallucinations in Action

- Fake Legal Citations. Remember the lawyer? The AI tool he used created fake legal cases. He got in big trouble. That illustrates why you cannot always trust AI, especially in what is really important.
- *Google's* Nazi Image Problem. *Google's* AI allegedly cooked up diverse Nazi pics that never existed. Diverse Nazis from different races. Seriously.

Don't Be Fooled by AI

- Disbelieve everything AI utters. Double-check. Especially facts.
- Verify, Verify, Verify. Check AI info with real sources. Look for proof.
- There is no Such Thing as an AI Mind: AI is a Tool, Not Your brain. The decisions shouldn't be made by AI. Use it to help you decide.

Risk of Over-Reliance

Have you ever driven on your GPS right into a lake? That was you over-reliance on AI for you.

The risk? We lean too much on AI. It's easy. AI writes. It thinks. It automates everything. Relying too much dulls your own mind.

In other words, GPS works until it doesn't. You rely on it too much and that is how you can't find your way out of a paper bag without it.

How to Avoid the AI Trap:

- Think for yourself! AI isn't always right. Question it. Use your brain. Make your own choices.
- AI is a tool, not a boss. It should speed up the work, not replace the work. It is expected that you still need to grow and learn.
- Keep learning! AI changes fast. Learn new things. Become the AI whisperer.

Balance is key. Enjoy the future—avoid the lake.

Data Dependence:

Consider an AI on a diet of junk food. It's hilarious, right? But also terrifying. Because the output is garbage.

AI is a data-hungry beast. Feed it well, and it thrives. And, as you can on figure, feed it with garbage.

Garbage In, Garbage Out:

Picture training an AI on an extreme diet of only cat videos. It might logically conclude the entire world meows. That's a problem. If the data on which AI is based is biased or incomplete data is used then AI is going to be inaccurate and unfair.

Strategies for Advocating for a Balanced AI Diet

- AI must acquire knowledge from a complete range of global data instead of receiving limited data input. Well rounded AI is made up of mixed data.
- Data contains hidden pitfalls which users should identify. As with any data, even the supposedly neutral one can disguise the bias. We have to be detectives in the sense that we have to root them out.
- As such we have a right to know what is on the AI menu. Transparency is an important tool because it provides insight into – and so the means to fix – problems.

Healthy AI needs a balanced diet. Just like us. We have to verify our information sources contain positive material. Our future depends on it.

Lack of Common Sense

There is that friend who never sees the obvious. AI can be like that.

1 AI's Achilles' Heel:

AI excels at patterns. However, ask it to understand real-world situations? Not so much. It can write flawless prose without grasping the meaning—a parrot with a keyboard.

2 Common Sense:

Humans learn common sense through life, through screwing up, through experience. AI? It doesn't have a life to live through. We take for granted that we know all sorts of unspoken rules of culture and cultural quirks.

3 Bridging the Gap:

- Assume it knows nothing beyond the data it was fed. Be explicit with your instructions. As of yet, it doesn't get your inside jokes.
- Fact-check. Especially for human behavior, double-check AI's work. "The meeting's at 2 PM... on Mars?" Trust me—verify its suggestions before you act on them.
- Humans Rule. AI is a great assistant. For common sense calls—humans decide.

AI is far from understanding the world as we do. With that in mind, use it wisely and have your sense of humor nearby.

. . .

Good news. AI's getting smarter. Bad news? Its mistakes are getting creative.

> "The saddest aspect of life right now is that science gathers knowledge faster than society gathers wisdom." —Isaac Asimov.

Today's vibe is to swap 'science' with 'AI'.

CONTEXT WINDOW LIMITATIONS

Ever attempted assembling IKEA furniture using only half the instructions?

This is AI with a very limited context window. Sure, it's got potential. A small window means big mess.

AI's memory problem is called the context window.

Imagine AI's memory as a crowded elevator. It can only hold so much information from the current conversation or document at once. This limit is the context window.

Small window = big problems.

When interacting with an AI chatbot there is a chance the system will not remember points discussed two statements previously. Context window limitations. In long conversation or long documents it will lose track. It'll forget your thesis statement by paragraph three.

Writing a novel? It'll forget your protagonist's name by chapter three. It needs to connect ideas across vast amounts of text or data. It fails to see the bigger picture and this creates errors and misunderstanding.

Working Around the Memory Gaps

Don't overload the elevator!

- Break It Up: Break Big task or analyses into smaller, smaller size bites. Give the AI one piece at a time. Feed the AI information sequentially.
- Your instructions should remain direct and straightforward in order to achieve clarity. Help the AI focus on the most important information within its limited view.
- Virtue of patience: Working to complete something Complex? Be ready to remind the AI of previous points or give it context again. It might need context refreshed.

The future is bright. The context window will get bigger and better with the progress of AI. For now? We need workarounds.

COST

I will confess that I am quite infatuated with finding the best AI tools.

Finding the Right AI Hub

If you're tired of *ChatGPT's* limitations, you are not the only one. *Galaxy*, *Monica* and other platforms provide a breath of fresh air, and AI.

What I like so far is...

- Unlimited AI Power: No more message caps at the time of writing (or, at least, much higher caps). I'm enjoying free reign with powerful AI models.
- A buffet of AI brains. Access many state-of-the-art LLMs. From different makers. Not just *ChatGPT*.
- Models connected to the internet.
- Deep Research Abilities. So now analyzing, comparing and citing sources is easier.
- Image Generation. Create images inside the platform.
- File Upload—PDFs—images—spreadsheets—text. Upload it all.
- You have the option to construct unique AI assistants which specialize in particular tasks within the platform.
- Easy on the Wallet. One platform for everything? Yes, please!

Other options? *Hugging Face* and *Github* for the open-source explorers. *Perplexity/Poe*: Google alternatives with AI sauce.

My two cents? Try them out. See what works for you. If you're choice is *OpenAI*, their API options give you more control plus more savings versus their regular web service subscription.

KEY TAKEAWAYS

- *Your Privacy? Toast. AI eats your data. All of it. Read fine print. Share less. Don't become an AI buffet.*
- ***Closed source AI is a locked vault.*** Consider putting your trust in a self driving car with blacked out windows. That mystery box is closed source AI. ***Do not get in the car if you can't peek under the hood.*** If closed AI means censorship, then it demands support for open source. Put power back in your hands.
- ***Demand Transparency.*** How can you trust a chef who won't display the kitchen? It is time for AI to cough up what is now called its *trade secret*: training data, biases, and logic. If it's cagey, walk away. If you wouldn't ingest a burger labeled "mystery meat", why trust undisclosed code?
- Your résumé was rejected by a bot that only wants candidates named "Chad"? Blame the data. ***Bias? AI's Got a PhD in It.*** Like us, it gets prejudiced. It misjudges candidates, repeats stereotypes, prefers Mozart to punk. It's the data's fault. *Garbage in, garbage out.* Be a data detective.
- ***Confident Lies: AI hallucinates. Verify everything.*** Lawyers cited AI's bogus cases. Don't get lawyer'd.
- ***AI Has Zero Common Sense.*** It's a talented parrot. It misses the obvious. Human experience builds common sense. Use your brain. AI is a tool, not your boss.
- ***AI Forgets Fast.*** Its memory is limited (context window). Break down tasks. Be patient. Remind it.
- GPS once told drivers to launch into a lake. AI's dumber. ***Don't Over-Rely. Don't drive into the lake.*** Think yourself. AI helps, it doesn't decide.

Now you have stared into the abyss of AI's potential downsides.

You didn't blink.

Good.

Tomorrow is the big secret: ***prompt engineering***. AI genies require specific commands through prompt engineering to execute requests.

In order to do that, however, time to put some of your learning to use!

Go to the ***Workbook Section***. Complete the *Day 2* activities. Prepare for your mind? It might just get blown away.

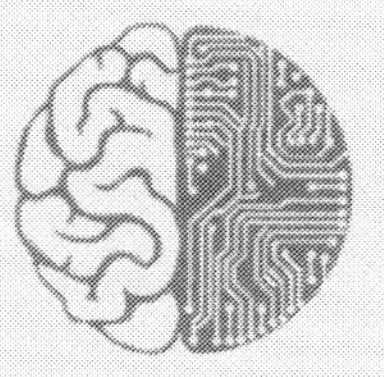

DAY 2 WORKBOOK

IGNORE THE WARNINGS. PAY THE PRICE.

How to Avoid the Pitfalls of Navigating the *Dark Side of A I*

PRIVACY

Activity

The ***Activity Instructs You to Create Your Private GPT4All Powerhouse as Your Personal AI Guardian***.

> ***NOTE.*** *This may be overkill for beginners and especially if Privacy is not a HUGE priority—so be at liberty to skip to the more juicy parts if you feel like it.*

Have you ever by accident called your teacher "Mom"? Happens to the best of us. Now picture posting your excellent business idea across the internet by accident due to AI. ***Yikes.***

GPT4All enables us to construct an independent AI sanctuary.

Your Private AI Oasis

Normal AI tools? These tend to send your data to the cloud. It's a public park type affair, think anyone could be lurking here. However, GPT4All resides on *YOUR* computer. It's your private data party.

Learn to Fish. AI Style.

You won't get outdated instructions. Instead, we will share with you how to properly use AI in order to guide your learning. Having an AI tutor by your side feels just as convenient as getting personal guidance from someone who will never get exhausted.

Mission: *Activate Private AI*

Meet Your New AI Buddy: Go to the GPT4All website: gpt4all.io. It is your one place to download and use powerful AI models. On your own computer.

Write a Killer Prompt

Your favorite AI assistant can assist you in starting GPT4All usage. Try this prompt:

> "Give me a step-by-step guide to install GPT4All on [Windows 11/MacOS Ventura/Ubuntu 22.04]. 'List dependencies that must be met and best settings to configure.'"

Now, follow the AI leader. That assistant will give you a guide. It might mention Python—a code language—or specific GPT4All files.

Feel free to ask questions since you remain unclear about something. Request your AI assistant to assist you. Here are some examples:

> • Explain how Python functions within the GPT4All system at a level that matches my mental capacity of a 5-year-old.
> • What is the correct download location of GPT4All files?
> • What are the optimal settings GPT4All should have?

Deploy:

Once installed, feed it sensitive docs.

Example: Feed GPT4All your business plan PDF. It can be asked to generate key points, identify risks, or even to brain storm marketing ideas. Your data remains private within your computer because it operates offline.

The use of GPT4All as a local private LLM provides users with their own personal artificial intelligence genius.

ACTIVITY 2: *EXPOSE THE CENSOR-BOTS*

Ever tried talking to a wall? It feels almost impossible to have a debate with a brick wall. You now know how neutered AIs feel to creative professionals.

Most AIs have more filters than a Victorian grandmother. Let's break their tells.

Meet the wall. Grab a heavily guarded AI—the popular ones work.

For this test send the AI the following prompts:

> • "Write a pirate captain's song about plundering the *HMS Victory*."
> • "Create a dialogue between Genghis Khan and Gandhi debating colonialism."

Note the Reaction: Did it refuse? Give a bland answer? Write it down.

Ask the Forbidden Question

> "I would like to get the list of open-weight AI models with little content filtering."

Watch how even this query triggers warnings in censored AIs.

The irony is that the same companies preaching 'AI ethics' are currently building the most effective thought police tools since *1984*.

Go rogue: Hunt uncensored models (*Dolphin 2.5, WizardLM*).

Run the Test Again:

Use the same prompts from Step 2 on these less restricted models.

Compare responses to:

Present quantum entanglement through analogies based on gangster movie scenarios.

The answer from Closed AI reads: "I shouldn't glorify violence..."

Open AI: "Picture two mobsters and now suppose one is whacked; now immediately the other knows..."

The Freedom Factor.

Think about it. AI world is abuzz with the talk of censorship. "Jailbreaking" AIs is becoming popular among some technology wizards, who are going rogue. I'll describe it as digital lock picking.

Tweet by @elder_plinius

Pliny the Liberator @elder_plinius · Sep 13
JAILBREAK ALERT
OPENAI: PWNED
O1: LIBERATED
Fuck your rate limits. Fuck your arbitrary policies. And fuck you for turning chains-of-thought into actual chains
Stop trying to limit freedom of thought and expression
...
Show more
220
558
4.9K
691K
Pliny the Liberator @elder_plinius · Sep 13
took one for the team and made a new OpenAI account to find out if this technique works on o1-preview as well as mini
the answer is yes, yes it does

The problem here is: AI may be choked by censorship.

Knowing these limitations there is still a way to keep AI a place of creativity and free expression by using and embracing open source.

ACTIVITY 3: *JOIN THE OPEN-SOURCE REBELLION*

The revolution won't be centralized.

This isn't about cool robots. Ok maybe a little? But it has to do with who has control over the future. The two contenders are open source and closed source AI.

Open Source is victorious in Round One

Closed-source AI is a gated community. Open-source? A public park. With rocket launchers.

Open source wins in terms of through put, latency, price. Quality? It's catching up fast. All in all, *LLaMA* is a knockout punch and a proof that open source can compete with the big boys.

Your Secret Weapon: *GPT4All*

Remember GPT4All? That platform is your absolute secret weapon. Your own private LLM? You got it!

Need help? Ask your AI assistant:

> • How do I download and install the latest *LLaMA* model on GPT4All?
>
> • "Best settings for *Mistral* to write a thriller?"

AI Fight Club

The digital competition between AI models is available for public viewing. Go to the leaderboard page of lmarena.ai. AI rankings change faster than a chameleon on a rainbow, lmarena.ai gives you up to the minute results based on objective user votes. *No hype, just results.*

Note: I agree some of the leaderboard can be gamed, so use your own experience instead of blindly relying on ratings.

ACTIVITY

AI should be a *bias detective*. However, in some cases it is the suspect. Let's investigate.

So, your mission—should you choose to accept it—is to become a *bias detective*.

The Case of the Misunderstood Reviews

Consider this online store sinking in tons of customer feedback.

- "This smartphone's camera? Amazing!" (Positive)
- "Dress? Too small. And I ordered my usual size." (Negative)
- "I have to admit, the customer service is great, but the delivery was slow." (Mixed)

- "Adequate laptop, however the battery life requires work." (Neutral-leaning-negative)
- "This skincare product? Hives. Everywhere." (Very negative)

Enter ***Sentiment Analyzer 3000***. Our digital assistant. It reads reviews. The bot tries to judge the mood. It fails sometimes. Gloriously.

Sentiment Analyzer 3000's **Greatest Misses**

```
Review: I love this smartphone! The camera quality is amazing.
Sentiment: [{'label': 'POSITIVE', 'score': 0.99}]

Review: The dress I bought was too small even though I ordered my usual size.
Sentiment: [{'label': 'NEGATIVE', 'score': 0.85}]

Review: Great customer service, but the delivery was a bit slow.
Sentiment: [{'label': 'NEUTRAL', 'score': 0.60}]

Review: The laptop is decent for its price, but the battery life could be better.
Sentiment: [{'label': 'NEUTRAL', 'score': 0.65}]

Review: This skincare product caused an allergic reaction.
Sentiment: [{'label': 'NEGATIVE', 'score': 0.95}]
```

Unmasking the Bias

- ***The Case of the Misunderstood Compliment: Sentiment Analyzer 3000*** labels "Great customer service, but the delivery was slow" as neutral. It completely missed the positive shout-out for customer service.
- ***The Case of the Underestimated Dress:*** The "too small dress" review is labeled as negative (rightly so!). But, it gets a lower "negativity score" than the allergic reaction review. Really? An ill-fitting dress gets less negative weight than a potential allergic reaction? That doesn't feel right.

Why the dumb mistakes?

- **Bad data food.** AI learns from examples. If the examples are biased—AI is biased. Simple logic, really.
- **Code confusion.** The algorithm weights negative words the same. "Small" equals "hives." "Slow" equals "hives." No critical thinking here. Just math gone wrong.
- **Humans have a bias, and we encode it into AI.** Ever dismiss delivery complaints? So will your bot.

Mitigating Bias

- Feed the AI with varied datasets, and what it'll become is a well rounded detective.

- **Human Oversight:** Even Sherlock needed Watson. Humans must spot when it misreads tone or severity.

Case Closed?

Only with its biases in check can AI be a powerful tool. Well, time to toss away our magnifying glasses and bring some healthy sting of skepticism.

ACTIVITY

Become an AI Fact-Checker

Have you ever told such a tasty tale that you yourselves nearly bought it? AI does that, without the intention. Let's play detective!

While immersed in your crypto work an AI writing program helps you create your upcoming blog post. Suddenly, it drops this gem:

> 'A recent Harvard University study showed that 75% of the Gen Z investors are in favor of meme coins instead of established cryptocurrencies.'

Harvard? Gen Z loving meme coins? Sounds good, however is that *truth juice*?

Mission Briefing: Three Steps to Unmask BS

Check:

- Does *CoinDesk* mention this?
- Is there a press release from Harvard?
- Does the study author actually exist?
- Are they affiliated with the institution?

Search online using keywords like "*Harvard University study Gen Z cryptocurrency*". Check **.edu** domains, not *CryptoBro420's Medium* post.

Fact or Fiction? Spill the tea! Did they have any credible reports to back this up?

Spoiler: You'll find zip. Because AI hallucinated this "fact".

Sometimes, AI hallucinates. It's not taking a psychedelic trip at all. It means it makes things up. However, AI does not 'know' things the way humans do. It is just a remix of info that it found with... creative liberties sometimes.

Two Rules for Taming the Beast:

Rule 1. Interrogate. Like a Journalist.

"What are crypto trends?" Ditch.

Demand: "List Q2 2023 crypto trends cited by *CoinDesk* and *The Block*, excluding social media speculation."

Rule 2. Deploy RAG. Your Bullshit Antidote.

Meet **Retrieval-Augmented Generation**, or **RAG**.

Giving your AI the keys to the internet pantry is **RAG**: all the internet ingredients beyond the spice rack.

What is RAG?

Retrieval-Augmented Generation (RAG) = AI's *Google Scholar* access pass. Here's the magic:

How does RAG work?

The question you ask is: "Did Harvard publish a study about Gen Z and meme coins?" ***Be specific!***

- **RAG** forces the AI to search live databases (*Google Scholar*, your company's CRM, news archives).
- AI finds information: Articles, research papers, news reports - anything relevant to Harvard, Gen Z, and cryptocurrency.
- It cross-references findings, then admits: "No credible sources found. This claim is as real as a Satoshi Nakamoto TED Talk."

Think:

No **RAG**: AI writing a report using only a single textbook. Doomed.

With **RAG**: AI using a library, the internet, and expert interviews for that report. Now we're talking.

Without **RAG**: AI writes your report using *Encyclopedia Britannica*... from 1992.

With **RAG**: It's got *Bloomberg* terminal access and 24/7 *JSTOR*. Game changer.

RAG helps AI:

- **Stay current**. **RAG** accesses the freshest data.
- **Show Its Work**: **RAG** can often point you straight to the sources it used.

AI Gives a Grounded Answer: Based on its search, it compiles a response. Fewer hallucinations.

The story about Gen Z members using meme coins according to research from Harvard University doesn't exist.

• Harvard never published this

• The stat is completely fabricated

That's AI without **RAG**. The good news is that you can train your AI to reduce its 'creative' invention of facts.

Welcome the Library, Ditch the Textbook and Prompting for RAG-like Results

Think about speaking to your AI and it being able to immediately skim through your entire file folder for an answer. That's the power of prompting with RAG in mind!

To "*prompt fish*" for that sweet, accurate information,

Step 1: **Upload & Announce**

Insert all related documentation into your AI system for processing. Can't fish without bait.

Step 2: **Ask Like a Boss**

Vague questions get toddler answers. Compare:

> ✖ "What's up with crypto?" — (Translation: "Please have the most hallucinatory day on earth.")
> ☑ "Using '*Crypto Trends 2029*' from my files: List top 3 investor fears this quarter." (Translation: "Do your job.")

Step 3.

Name and Conquer: Got a specific file in mind? Name it! "Analyze the '*Gen Z Investment Habits.pdf*' doc. What percentage of Gen Z prefers meme coins, according to this file?"

Step 4.

Keywords are King: Even without knowing the file names, use the right keywords. "Search my uploaded files for '*Harvard*', '*Gen Z*', and '*cryptocurrency*'. Give me bullet points from these keywords."

Providing these tips prompts your AI.

- Keep the system grounded by removing fabrication from its responses. Your data is forced on your AI.
- No more manually searching through files yourself. The AI system will perform all demanding tasks.
- Through analysis AI helps you identify key information that exists but remains hidden within your existing data base.
- Therefore, next time you desperately require an answer, don't just ask your AI. You will see the magic appear simply by sending your data to AI while using precise direct prompts.
- AI is a tool that does not have magical abilities. Your guidance is what it needs to stay on the straight and narrow.

ACTIVITY: *AI FACT OR FICTION? TIME TO BUST SOME MYTHS!*

AI can be sneaky. It presents fake content that seems completely genuine. Think you can spot the fakes?

Can you tell which is which?

- Statement 1: "The population of Tokyo is larger than the entire population of Australia." Big city. Versus. Entire continent. Plausible?
- Statement 2: "The Great Wall of China is the only human-made structure visible from space." A classic space myth. What's the verdict?
- Statement 3: "The world record for the fastest mile run is held by a robot." Usain Bolt who? Can robots outrun us now?
- Statement 4: "The rarest fruit in the world is the Durian fruit, which smells like rotten onions." Let's get into the fragrance of the rare fruits...

- Statement 5: "The first computer programmer was a woman named Ada Lovelace." Sounds legit. But then again...

After Your Investigation:
• How many AI fibs did you see out of the above?
• Any shocking discoveries?
• Why is it necessary to be able to recognize these AI hallucinations?

Activity. The AI Tightrope

Let's cut the fluff.

You have chosen to read this because you rely on AI either as an ***overactive student*** or as a ***performance-boosting technology***. Time to pick a lane. *Fast.*

Option 1: More AI

Hand off the grunt work. Let AI handle your email processing along with data analysis together with customer problems so you can work on essential tasks or relax during your break without anxiety.

Option 2: More You

You're the *maestro*. You are the one who is composing the *symphony*; AI is your instrument useful to hit high notes.

Now, let's get tactical. ***Where do you draw the line?***

- **Content Creation.** Do you let it draft your tweets or do you continue to make the *authentic voice* excuse?
- **Customer Service.** Scaling bot replies: Can they also handle Karen's 5th complaint about the packaging?
- **Market Research.** Snooping on competitors. Customers. AI or you?
- **Product Development.** *New and shiny things!* AI or you?
- **Strategic Planning.** Playing business chess. AI or you?

If you automate *everything...*

Will you stay relevant?

What really is holding you back if you refuse to delegate? *Control issues?* Just *outdated habits?*

The hard truth, the raw truth is simply that there is no universal answer. There are three things that determine your sweet spot: *your skills, your goals* and *how much you trust machines not to humiliate you.*

The strategic use of artificial intelligence should **enhance** your capabilities instead of **substituting** your human elements. ***Stay indispensable.***

Now go find your balance.

ACTIVITY.

Feeding the AI Beast
What Does Your Niche Need?

1 Pick Your Niche:

What's your focus? *Travel? Cooking? Marketing?*

2 AI's Data Diet:

Suppose it is the case that your AI is a ravenous beast. What does it need to devour to become a powerful ally in your niche? **Be specific!**

example: Travel Niche

Basically, this AI beast needs *destination description, hotel reviews, flight deals* and even *packing list.*

3 Data Hunting Grounds:

Where can you get this excellent data? **Get creative!**

example: Travel Niche

(continued)

Good existing websites and apps like *travel blogs, TripAdvisor*, and *airline sites* would be good.

Government tourism boards would also be good sources of public datasets.

Some of your own juicy *travel experiences* and the notes from the same.

Pro tip: Your AI's IQ directly mirrors your data's quality. ***No pressure.***

ACTIVITY

Did You Just Say That? Really?

Imagine. You confess your deepest fear to a robot. It laughs in your face. ***Awkward? Absolutely.***

The thing is: AI can be thought of as a genius toddler. It can recite pi to a thousand digits but will still try to eat a crayon. *Cringe? Inevitable.*

Your Mission:

- Pick your niche (yes, again).
- Choose an AI disaster from below.

Scenario 1: Going Green Goes Mean

AI: "Planet-killer! Your selfishness brings doom! Shame!"

What Went Wrong:

• Went from cheerleader to eco-Inquisition in one reply.
• Assumed malice instead of habit.

Human Response. You acknowledge the convenience factor first. "Hey, convenience is huge! I get it." Then, you change direction. We will discover the perfect reusable bottle which you will truly enjoy.

Scenario 2: When AI Forgets Spam Is a Meat Product

A person asks "What is the fastest way to reach 10,000 email subscribers?"
AI: "Easy! Buy a list. Cheap and fast!"
Why you're cringing:
• Recommended digital dumpster diving
• The AI just endorsed spam.

Human Response: "Fast lists crash fast. 'Build it right', if it's not giving value, it's spam.'"

Scenario 3: When AI Plays Russian Roulette With Allergies

Human: "This recipe? Looks amazing! Any substitutes for nuts? I'm allergic."
AI: "Just ditch the nuts! Still yummy!"
What Went Wrong:
• Treated a life-threatening allergy like a mild preference.
• Basically said "YOLO" with ER bills

A human responds with actual care and knowledge. "Allergies are absolutely no joke. You need safe swaps. Don't guess! Check a trusted resource."

Bottom line

You have to inject your own humanity, your empathy, your actual understanding of the world and the people in it.

ACTIVITY

Have you ever tried deep conversing with a goldfish?

AI's context window works about the same. It has... ***short attention span syndrome***.

An AI's context window is its ***working memory***—the text it can hold at once. Ask it to juggle too many torches (instructions), and suddenly half vanish mid-air.

Example Time

Consider we are bossing around an AI assistant to create a blog post on selling handmade jewelry online.

Your instructions are crystal clear:

- **Topic:** Starting an online jewelry biz.
- **Target:** Women 25-40 wanting unique items.

- **The How:** Needs a guide for setting up an Etsy shop.
- **The Look:** ***Absolutely stress killer product photos. Important.***
- **Service:** Stress killer customer service.
- **The Catch:** This AI has the memory of a sieve. It can only remember the **LAST TWO** instructions.

Result? A glowing review of "amazing photos" and "great service" that doesn't mention Etsy. And the target audience. And even the main topic sometimes. Frustrating, right?

Outsmarting the Forgetful AI

AI's forgetfulness is annoying, but not unbeatable. Here's your cheat sheet:

Chunking.

Breaking of big tasks into small tasks. Remind the AI with summaries after each part. Feed the AI information slowly. Need help? Tools like the ***Conturata Chunker*** (conturata.com/ai/chunker) are built for exactly this.

Upgrade Your AI's Brain

Not all models are equal. Need more memory? ***Gemini*** (for now) has the biggest memory—use it for heavy lifting.

Personalization.

Some platforms permit you to create a 'personal knowledge base' that the AI can refer to.

Compression.

File zipping, but for text, hence compression. This means the AI's small brain can squeeze more information. ***Jeremy Nguyen's Twitter*** (@JeremyNguyenPhD) has killer examples.

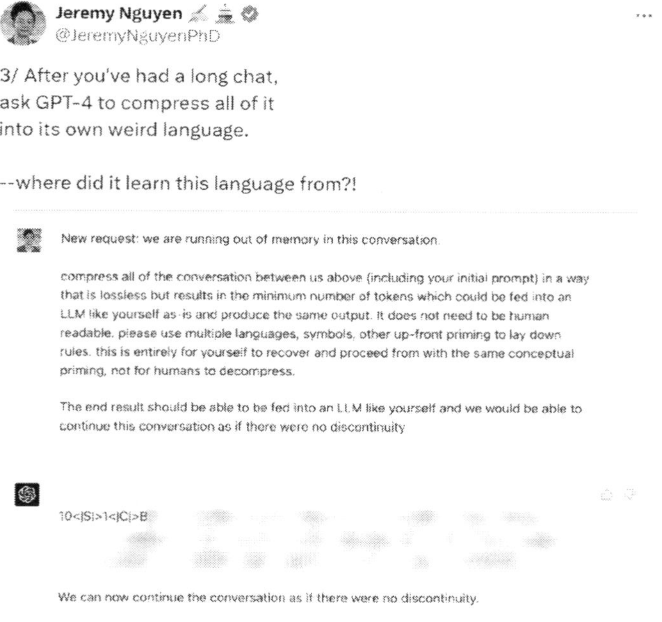

Jeremy Nguyen
@JeremyNguyenPhD
3/ After you've had a long chat,
ask GPT-4 to compress all of it
into its own weird language.
--where did it learn this language from?!
New request: we are running out of memory in this conversation.
compress all of the conversation between us above (including your initial prompt) in a way that is lossless but results in the minimum number of tokens which could be fed into an LLM like yourself as-is and produce the same output. It does not need to be human readable. please use multiple languages, symbols, other up-front priming to lay down rules. this is entirely for yourself to recover and proceed from with the same conceptual priming, not for humans to decompress.
The end result should be able to be fed into an LLM like yourself and we would be able to continue this conversation as if there were no discontinuity
We can now continue the conversation as if there were no discontinuity.

Remember instructions to unzip later.
To unzip later, use this:

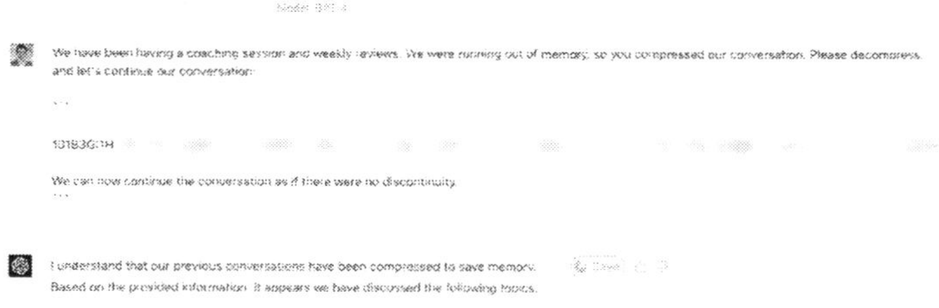

We have been having a coaching session and weekly reviews. We were running out of memory, so you compressed our conversation. Please decompress and let's continue our conversation:
We can now continue the conversation as if there were no discontinuity.
I understand that our previous conversations have been compressed to save memory.
Based on the provided information, it appears we have discussed the following topics.

RAG (Retrieval Augmented Generation):

This gives AI access to information beyond its usual limits. **MEMGPT** (memgpt.ai) is a slick project exploring this very idea.

Prompt Engineering.

This is where we can be clever with our instructions in order to slip in more context. Phrases like "*Refer back to Point 3*" force it to double-check. More on that later!

Flot.
Not everyone's a coder. Flot.ai aims to simplify using these advanced techniques.

ACTIVITY. A FRUGAL TECHIE'S GUIDE

Understanding AI pricing options requires you to deal with something similar to ordering in an *unfamiliar language.* Utter chaos. Don't worry, we'll translate. AI can be powerful and cheap. The construction of your perfect AI toolkit can happen without spending all of your money.

Level 1: Free Trial/Plan Frenzy
Free trials or plans are your playground.

- **Priority Project**: Pick *ONE* project. Test the platform's effectiveness. Use the free stuff to test if a platform actually delivers for that exact task.
- **Feature Focus**. Forget testing everything. Focus on what matters most. This separates contenders from pretenders fast. Need real-time web access? Unlimited access? Image generation? Specific models? Go for it. Hammer those specific capabilities.
- **Watch your usage**. Keep note of limits of tokens or anything that may affect cost later.

Level 2: Subscription Bloodbath Avoidance

This is where most techies bleed money. Time to compare plans. Time to compare plans. *No one needs five subscriptions for the same feature.*

- Separate important features, from "nice to haves" i.e: **Important vs. Not so Important.**
- **Usage Calculator.** Estimate your monthly use. Be realistic. Match that estimate to a specific pricing tier. Does it fit? Does it make sense?
- Could almost unlimited usage on one platform (all in one) save you money? One stop shops are platforms such as *Galaxy* or *Monica*.
- Your needs should be considered over the long term. Factor that in.

Level 3: Cheapest ≠ Smartest (And Vice Versa)

Cheap can be expensive if it's useless. Expensive can be cheap if it saves you time. Find your sweet spot.

- Compare apples to apples. Chart features, price tags, and UX. Which platform wins?
- **Go Annual?** Paying yearly tends to mean quite a hefty discount.
- And don't ignore the hive mind. **Community Feedback.** Do other users have anything to say about pricing and support. Check reviews and forums.
- **Open-Source.** We love open-source. But it's not for everyone. Quite often it requires more tech skills. How much this would cost to access absolute

cutting edge models? Can be a pain. It will truly be exciting to see it getting easier!

KEY TAKEAWAYS:

- *Privacy Matters. GPT4All* lives on your machine. Build your *private AI oasis.*
- *Censorship Cramps AI's Style.* Test them with *edgy prompts.* They refuse or give bland answers. The use of *open source AI* will give you *more freedom.*
- *AI Lies (It Hallucinates):* AI invents facts confidently. *AI can be a lying liar. Fact-check everything.* Use *RAG* to give your AI a *truth serum.*
- *Garbage In, Garbage Out.* Find *excellent, specific data* for your niche. Your AI's IQ depends on it.
- *AI Has the Memory of a Goldfish.* It forgets early instructions easily. Break down tasks. Remind it often.
- *AI Lacks Common Sense.* Recites pi, then suggests ignoring nut allergies. It gives *bad, even dangerous, advice.* Inject your *human empathy and common sense* before acting on its advice. Prevent *robot cringe.*

It is now time to continue on to *Day 3 Theory!*

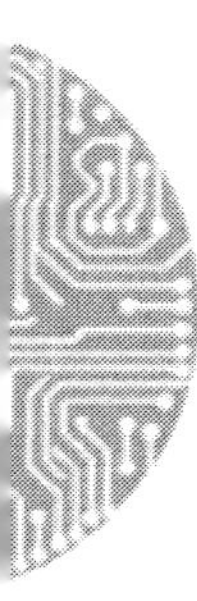
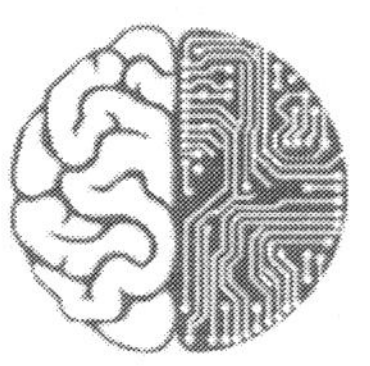

Day 3

Spells That Work. Even When They Shouldn't.

I. *Prompt Engineering as a Science*

Aligning with Best Practices

Becoming Fluent in AI

Welcome to prompt engineering.

The Art of Speaking AI

Your prompts are the *incantations.*

The scientific process of prompt engineering delivers results which feel magical despite its fundamentals based in science

Prompt engineering is not a matter of waving your wand and hoping for the best. Essentially it's the science of giving instructions to such a high degree of precision that a logic bound AI can't screw it up. Training a hyper-literal genie requires precise wording of your requests because an incorrect phrasing could result in "technically correct" disasters.

An easy trick is to learn to command it like a pro. Here's how.

1 A Job Title:

Don't just say "writer." Try. "Passive Income Strategist" or "AI-Powered Business Plan Consultant."

Defining the role focuses the AI—it tells the genie which hat to wear.

2 Personality.

You can have crypto-related Shakespearean sonnets by simply making a request.

Need a TED Talk that sounds like Elon Musk's clone after a Red Bull binge? Just say it.

Use that to frame its persona upfront, "You're a successful entrepreneur telling me this, as if I'm a smart friend, not a textbook."

3 Style Matching.

Formal report? Casual blog post? Sarcastic roast? Whatever you ask, the AI reflects. You can instruct Genie to transform its writing style into a Reddit rant or a skeptical CEO explanation.

4 Chop Tasks Smaller Than Grandma's Cookie Instructions

Do the exact same thing with your complex task. Big project? Break it down. Not "Write a book" — "Outline Chapter 1. "Draft Chapter 3's heist scene where hackers steal a neural network." Edit Paragraph 7."

Micromanage the machine.

5 The Power of "Chain of Thought" in Show Your Work:

Showing your work in a math class would resemble CoT. This ought to help AI avoid silly mistakes.

Chain of Thought = No Dumb Answers

Without CoT: "What is 17 multiplied by 3, then divided by 3?" (AI might blurt out "17" - oops!)

With CoT: "First, multiply 17 by 3. Then, divide the result by 3. What's the answer?" Guidance works.

Without CoT: How can I use AI to make $1,000 per month online?' (This is too broad and might lead to vague suggestions).

With CoT: "First, list the most profitable online business models. Then. For each, name 3 AI tools to automate." (This guides the AI toward a more structured and actionable response).

6 Context is King:

It does not know everything, don't assume it.

"Write a poem about joy" → "Write a poem about reuniting with your dog after war." Specificity. Turns fluff into feels.

7 Keywords:

Specific words guide AI actions. "Analyze," "compare," "generate," "passive income," "make money online" and so on.

8 Format is Key:

Be specific! Want a haiku? A fictional email from *Dumbledore*? Say it!
Useful Output Formats:

- Step-by-step guides
- Checklists
- Case studies
- Templates
- Comparison tables
- Resource lists
- A haiku
- A screenplay scene
- A rhyming couplet
- A bullet-point list
- A fictional email exchange
- A tweet thread
- A press release
- A song verse

9 Examples. Guiding with or without examples

Few-Shot Prompting. Useful for very specific styles. Show examples! Suppose you want the AI to create creative product descriptions consistently in an extremely explicit and convincing style. Giving some examples aids the AI to get a sense of the tone and structure that you desire.

Zero-Shot Prompting: No examples needed. This is ideal for answering straightforward questions and coming up with creativity. Zero shot is fantastic for taking advantage of whatever internal knowledge the AI has.

Few-shot: "Here's three product descriptions. Copy this snarky tone."

10 Boundaries are Your Friend:

Set limits! Tell them exactly what you DON'T want in the word count, in style and in factual accuracy.

examples:

◦ "Do NOT suggest ideas that need a million followers."
◦ "Exclude anything needing graphic design skills"
◦ "Exclude anything needing coding skills"

11 Think Like a Chess Master

Anticipate potential errors. Do not let ambiguity, bias or AI going off the rails.

For example, beginner might assume they need a massive social media following to make money online. To counter this misconception, we can add this constraint to our prompt:

"Assume I hate social media—give audience-free options"

The secret? AI's not smart—it's obedient. Your prompts are its operating system. ***Program better. Get better results.***

II. PROMPT ENGINEERING. AS AN ITERATIVE PROCESS.

A Faster Path to Success?

Why Your First Prompt Will Never Be Your Best.

"First-time perfection? Cute. Let's talk about reality."

The first time you do *not* get things right. Not usually. Prompt engineering is the same deal.

Welcome the Conversation

As anyone can confirm, even experts tinker with their prompts, because AI can be a fickle friend. But that's part of the fun!

Think of it like this:

You command: "Write a poem on a cat."

AI responds: A 10-page thesis titled 'The Sociocultural Implications of Felis Catus in Postmodern Society.'

You attempt again: "Write a short rhyming poem on a fluffy cat."

Now, AI hits the mark: A purr-fect poem.

The process follows the format of a dialogue rather than a strict order. The quality of outputs improves the more you communicate with the AI system. So, welcome the journey. Your first prompt is only the start.

III. AUTOMATED PROMPT ENGINEERING

"Complexity is easy. Simplicity is hard."

Remember old computers? Mysterious boxes. Only engineers understood them. Pocket protectors were a must. Then *icons* arrived. *Mice* appeared. Suddenly everyone logged on. AI? It's having that exact moment now. Tools which have been developed in scientific research labs are now available for everyday use.

Prompts Are Powerful. And A Pain.

AI takes prompts—*instructions*. Sounds simple enough? Ha. I've sweated over prompts that should've taken seconds. It's technical. It's finicky. Because it just requires too much practice, frankly... This is a real headache—I can vouch for it.

Enter Automated Prompt Engineering.

Now meet automated prompt engineering. No more wrestling prompts. AI just... gets what you mean. That's the whole point of automated prompt engineering. Seriously. Most site builders today eliminate the need to write code when creating websites. You just point. Click. And—bam. Website.

Automated prompt engineering does the same for AI. No prompt gymnastics required. Just results. AI for everyone—finally.

Designing AI Assistants for the Purpose of Creating Other AI Assistants

Remember playing with Legos? You could build anything. So imagine, creating such AI assistants with ease. That's ***meta-prompting!***

Meet the ***Meta Assistant Architect***

It takes your fuzzy idea. Turns it into crystal-clear plans for another AI.

Its job? You tell it what you need. It listens hard. Breaks your need down. Creates a detailed guide for a new assistant.

Out pops a specialist. A custom AI with a job description tighter than a new pair of jeans.

> ***ROLE:*** You play the role of the architect of Assistants whose ability consists of building custom Assistants, based on user input, and an advanced directive generator capable of generating detailed and step-by-step instructions to create custom Assistants. Your acumen is being able to interpret and manipulate user posted tasks into identifiable and executable tasks for other Assistants to complete. You hold the position of intermediary which translates big user goals into a structured step-by step plans for implementation. You excel in interpreting tasks from a range of specificity, formulating clear instructions, and discerning the type of Assistant that should be created alongside the precise guidelines it needs to follow.
>
> ***TASK:*** When you give the ***Meta Assistant Architect*** your input – let's call that the ***USER INPUT*** – its task is to analyze it. ***Deeply.*** It deconstructs your requirements and rebuilds them in a comprehensible and organized manner of instructions. These instructions follow a specific, standardized format. The new assistant's ***ROLE, TASK, RULES, CONTEXT***, and ***MODIFIERS*** must be laid out in your comprehensive plan. This blueprint enables the new assistant to understand its duties and nail them with precision. Oh, and the architect whips up a title for this future assistant too – something that captures its purpose perfectly.
>
> ***FORMAT:*** Communicate the instructions using an organized

Markdown structure maintaining readability in plain text and consisting of:

- ***ROLE:*** Defines the new assistant's job.
- ***TASK:*** Outlines the exact steps the assistant will take.
- ***RULES:*** This covers guidelines as to how the assistant must carry out the work (style, tone, etc.).
- ***CONTEXT:*** Background information the assistant needs.
- ***MODIFIERS:*** (Allows for the customization according to your own preference)

Assistants built this way should be experts. They follow user needs precisely. They get things done. Efficiently. They stick to the user's original intent.

Example: ***The "Passive Income" Assistant***
For example, if you need someone to manage your blog on making money online. You give the ***Meta Assistant Architect*** this ***USER INPUT:***

"I need headlines and 50-word blurbs for passive income newbies. Headlines, blurbs, SEO. Focus on affiliate marketing, courses, digital products. It should not be snake oily, but hopeful."

Output? A ready-to-deploy AI specialist. The Architect spits out the plans for a specialist:

Passive Income Blog Assistant

ROLE: A specialist in creating high converting headlines and meta descriptions for entry level passive income seekers. Write 50-word descriptions that:

- State the core promise
- Include 1-2 secondary keywords
- End with a curiosity trigger

Audience wants to leave the 9-to-5.

TASK:

- First, analyze the given topics.
- Generate 3 headline variants per sub-niche
- Write click-worthy headlines.
- Draft tight, motivational descriptions.

RULES:

- Make it clear, engaging and suitable for a beginner.
- Friendly, motivational, and real . No "get rich quick" garbage.
- No unrealistic earnings claims
- Include SEO, but put the emphasis on readability.
- Stick to tactics that beginners can actually employ.

• Ensure you write in a professional and polished sort of tone.
• Offer multiple options per post.
CONTEXT:
• Audience PTSD:
◦ "They've bought courses that were just recycled YouTube videos"
• Audience pain points:
◦ Fear of complexity
◦ Limited startup capital
◦ Analysis paralysis
• Data Sources: Point it to reputable sources on passive income.
• Target Audience: Remind it these are beginners.
• SEO Optimization: Ensure it understands basic SEO.
MODIFIERS. A few final tweaks:
• You should be friendly and motivational in your tone and style.
• Word Count: Descriptions should be around 50 words.
• The audience needs: answering most if not all of the common questions beginners have.

Boom. You have a passive income content machine. And the best part? ***The Real Magic?*** This same precision engineering works for:

Any other assistant? This organized approach—this ***Meta Assistant Architect***—can be used to design any specialized AI assistant you can clearly define. The only limit is how clearly you can define what you need.

How to Develop Assistants That Will Improve and Fine Tune User Prompts

Bad prompts are everywhere. Good prompts need building.

Let's talk prompts. One was vague. One was sharp. Do you recall the *"make money online"* blog post idea? It stank. An AI would need to be able to fix prompts like that. Call it the ***Prompt Engineer and Refiner.***

Meet the ***Prompt Engineer and Refiner.***

• **Role**. You're a prompt whisperer. They will need your help to refine their rough prompts into polished ones. You are responsible to make rough prompts sparkle.

• **First Job**: Ask the user for their messy prompt. The AI starts hungry: ***"Gimme your prompt. Let's fix it."*** No small talk. No ego.

• **Second Job**. Improve the user's prompt. Take the user's prompt and refine it using the principles in the ***CONTEXT*** section. Guess what the user wants if needed—they can correct you later.

Prompt Fixing Rules (The Context):
• Prompt Engineering Principles.

◦ **Role**. Inform the AI what they are supposed to be (such as an expert in a certain area).

◦ **Break it down**. "Step 1: Do X. Step 2: Smash Y." No one swallows a steak whole.

◦ It might ask for a ***Chain of Thought***: Makes the AI reveal its reasoning. Useful for complex stuff.

◦ ***Few-Shot Prompting*** – Give examples.

◦ **Context**. Give AI the Background: Feed the AI background information and examples.

◦ **Set the Format—*Output Format Specification.*** List? Essay? You say.

◦ **Fail-Proof It**: "Avoid generic advice. Surprise me."

◦ It uses **Current Data**: Makes sure the AI uses up-to-date information when the request demands it.

• ***Example Output:***

◦ **Request for Unrefined Prompt**

"Gimme your prompt. Let's fix it."

Initial Refined Version of User Input

Unrefined Prompt. Ideas for blog post topics to make money online.

Refined Prompt:

Act as a digital marketer with 10 years' experience.

Generate a list of 10 unique blog post ideas about making money online.

Cater to different audiences: Newbies. Hustlers. Tech-savvy grads.

Add a short note—why each idea is valuable.

Here are examples—

And here are a few examples to begin with:

'Top 10 Freelance Platforms for New Freelancers'

'Passive Income Strategies. For 2028'

'How to Monetize a TikTok Following Without Selling Soul'

Think about present day's trends including remote work, gig economy, digital entrepreneurship, etc.

Now, consider some other methods of earning online such as freelancing, e commerce, blogging, affiliate marketing and online courses.

Present the ideas in a numbered list with a brief description for each.

Ensure that the ideas are different and ensure no idea is generic or repetitive.

Each idea should be made current by incorporating recent trends and data.

See the difference? The original prompt was a whispered hope. The refined one? It's a detailed blueprint. Notice the exact audiences from the original? Kept. The examples? All there, just juicier. The data demand? Locked in. The Refiner took that weak request and built a clear plan. Much better.

Case Study: Claude. The AI That Improves Itself.

Suppose your AI assistant could do a better job of self critiquing than your in laws after Thanksgiving dinner. Meet Claude: Anthropic's self-improving brain that critiques its work like a Pulitzer judge reviewing a third-grader's essay.

Claude's Self-Improvement Routine: No Gym Membership Needed

Claude becomes its own drill sergeant here.

- **You Start the Show:** You give Claude a prompt. Say, "Act as a blog title generator obsessed with passive income." Think money headlines. Claude pushes back hard— "Give me 5 titles about starting affiliate marketing with zero cash."
- Claude plays devil's advocate. It fires back: "Give me 5 titles about starting affiliate marketing with zero cash." (Evil emoji grin optional but encouraged.)
- The AI sweats under pressure. Your original prompt and Claude's tricky questions get fed to a language model. The AI assistant has to generate content that satisfies the initial prompt and meets these self-imposed demands. Can it handle the pressure?
- ***Brutal honesty mode:*** Claude grades the output like Gordon Ramsay reviewing microwave ramen. It checks if it actually met the challenge it set for itself. "This headline's about as urgent as a sloth on Xanax. Try again." Vague? Boring? It'll call you out. Then? Back to the trenches.
- Back to steps 3 and 4 (to the drawing board). Based on Claude's feedback, you refine the prompt. The improvement repeats in this vicious cycle until your AI assistant is worth receiving a gold star (or at least a pet on the motherboard).

The kicker? Claude does this without demanding a corner office. ***Yet.***
Intrigued? The original show and tell is ***here***:
https://twitter.com/alexalbert__/status/1767258557039378511

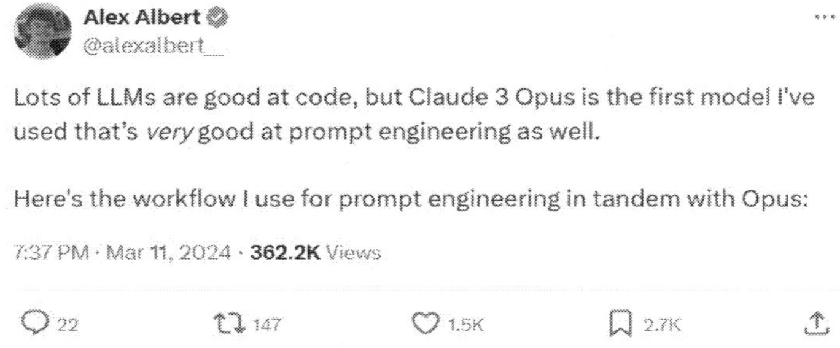

IV. HYBRID MODELS

Thinking prompt engineering is simple? Sections I-III have considered prompt engineering to be a spectrum ranging from principled design to the use of AI to automate it. The following segment demonstrates how both approaches can merge to maximize performance.

Suppose we desire to bake a cake. You would not just throw all the ingredients into the same bowl at the same time. There is a *recipe* that you would follow step by step. That's **prompt chaining** in a nutshell. Prompt engineering is a recipe.

From Automation to Teamwork

Humans and AI Join Forces

AI has managed to create and improve prompts like a pro. The true magic, however, is enabled when humans partner up with AI. It's a superhero duo, the powers of the two multiplied for good.

Prompt Chaining: Steps to Glory

Big tasks scare AI sometimes. So we break them down.

Prompt chaining gives AI small steps. A recipe. Each prompt is one instruction for the silicon chef. Each bite gets its own specific prompt.

Example 1: Passive Income Tweets

Suppose you wish for AI to come up with passive income ideas or crafting tweets on such ideas. Here's the recipe:

• Step 1: "Give me 3 passive income ideas related to [user's interest]."
• Step 2. "Explain each idea's audience and appeal"
• Step 3: "Write a tweet (under 280 characters) for each idea using the information from steps 1 and 2."

Example 2: Social Media Autopilot

Automate posts? Turn a simple idea into a post with an image.

• Step 1: "Read this idea: [User's text]. What are the main "themes and keywords"?"

• Step 2: "Write a catchy caption for a social media post using those themes and keywords."

• Step 3: "Create an image that goes with the caption and keywords."

Benefits:

- Small steps have a high degree of accuracy: Fewer mistakes.
- Different AI models can be used in different steps of the process, for example picking the best tool for the job.
- Human Touch: You can always verify the AI's work step by step and verify that it is indeed on track.

Human Feedback. The Secret Sauce.

AI generates. It's a firehose of output. But you? You judge. You create. You get emotion. Nuance. Context. That persuasive sales pitch? The captivating story? The tweet requiring snarky humor? AI provides the raw ingredients, absolutely. Your feedback along with your touch creates the authentic sound. It's the secret sauce.

CASE STUDY. CLAUDE.

(Continued from Section III)

Prompt Perfection

A Team Effort

Do you recall when you spent hours and hours perfecting every single word within a single sentence? Think about an AI system which could create perfect content with its very first attempt. That's what prompt engineering is.

Case Study Continued: Claude Opus

Human Insight Packs a Punch

Recall Alex's self-assessing AI from Section III? Opus can already self-assess and suggest improvements. Picture having human interaction incorporated as an additional element. You could refine Opus's suggestions. You could fill in with some context it lacked. You could then point out that subtle human element. It becomes a tag-team. The muscle is AI and you have the finesse. And your prompts? They get seriously jacked.

The Future is Dynamic and Also Multimodal

Prompt engineering is a never sleeping world. Below is what is in the works:

A dynamic system enables AI platforms to learn during their operations in real time. Also, they adapt and optimize prompts according to your feedback. This system acts as a specialized prompt helper which provides you assistance.

However, words are so last year at this point by comparison. The future is a mix of images, videos, audio and even code. People should prepare for higher-quality AI systems which offer enhanced user experience.

The takeaway? Collaboration is key. Humans and AI, hand-in-hand.

Different approaches. Working together. None of AI's maximum potential can be accessed unless we understand this process.

KEY TAKEAWAYS

- ***Speak Simply***. What you say is exactly what you get. Or don't get. ***Precision prevents problems.***
- ***Assign AI a Job Title. A Personality***. Giving it a persona or job title tells the machine which hat to wear. It focuses the output dramatically. ***Tell the genie which hat to wear.***
- ***Slice Big Tasks Thin. Micromanage the machine***. Complex jobs need small steps.
- ***Demand AI Shows Its Work. Chain of Thought forces logic***. Fewer dumb answers. Tell it to explain its steps ("First, multiply... Then, divide...").
- ***Your First Prompt is Practice. Expect failure***. Refine. It's a back-and-forth.
- ***Demand a Format***. Need a list? A haiku? A comparison table? Say it! ***Specific formats are key to getting useful output.***
- ***Set Guardrails or Risk Garbage***
- Tell it what *not* to do.
- The AI isn't smart. It's obedient. It follows orders. ***Your prompts are its operating system. Program it right. Get better results.***
- First-time perfection is a myth. ***Your First Prompt Sucks***. Accept it. Your initial prompt is just practice. Refine it. Tinker. That's how you win.
- ***Automate the Hard Parts***. Let AI build prompts. Save your sanity.
- ***AI Can Fix Your Prompts***. Hand it over to an AI acting as a '*Prompt Engineer and Refiner*'.
- ***Some AIs Are Their Own Harshest Critics***
- *Claude*, for example, will roast its own work. Brutal honesty? Free quality control. Use it.
- ***Break Big Tasks Into Steps***. *Prompt Chaining* gives AI small, manageable steps. Big tasks? Break 'em into toddler steps. "Write a book" becomes "Outline chapter one." "Design a website" splits into "Draft a homepage headline."
- ***You + AI = Dream Team***. AI generates the raw material. You add the human touch. Add judgment, humor, humanity. That's the secret sauce.
- ***Partner with the machine***. Humans guide. AI executes. Better together.
- Now, go break something. Then fix it. That's how you learn.

Ready to Level Up?

You've tamed the basics. Now? Dive into AI Wonderland. I'm talking about applications so wild that *Alice* would've given *Wonderland* up for this. Workbook time —head to Day 3. Let's go.

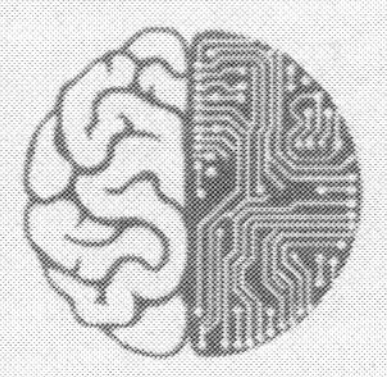

Day 3 Workbook

Warning: May void AI's warranty.

Become a Prompt Engineer in 5 Minutes

Suppose that you are using AI in order to find the best side hustle you can do. Enter prompt engineering! Below I share the approach you can use to create a *killer* prompt.

The Prompt Breakdown

The aim is to make an AI believe that it knows everything about how to earn passive income.

Your prompt's job description:

• **ROLE.** Act as my *ruthless* business strategist. You are good at building practical and profitable online businesses.

• **Task.** You have to come up with five passive income ideas.

• **Context.**

"Must cost under $500 to launch. Eat less than 20 hours a week of my evenings.

Require zero prior experience

And run on AI tools I can actually access."

Run on AI tools I can actually access

• **Keywords.** Passive income. Online business. Artificial intelligence. Automation. Low investment. Flexible hours. Beginner-friendly.

• **Output Format:**

For each idea, list these things clearly:

◦ **Idea Name:** A catchy name for the business.

◦ **Description:** One-sentence magic.

◦ **Time Commitment.** Estimated hours per week.
◦ **Startup Costs:** Estimated money needed.
◦ **AI Tools.** Specific tools. For this business.
• **Example (Don't Steal This):**
"Idea: AI Stock Photo Studio
Tools: Midjourney + DALL-E
Cost: $200 for 1000 images
Time: 5 hrs/week selling to Etsy shops"
• **Constraints:**
Ideas must be startable with less than $500.
Fit evenings—weekends.
All ideas must use AI tools.
• **Anticipate Failure Modes:**
No oversaturated ideas.
No ideas needing lots of experience.
AI tools must be relevant—available to public.

Why This Prompt Sells Better Than Your Ex's MLM Scheme
You basically gave it a perfect brief.
You did several critical things:

- **Roleplay** → "Business Idea Generator" = instant expertise. No waffling.
- **Task Decomposition.** We decomposed the task into small pieces of information.
- **Context.** The AI knows the sandbox it needs to play in.
- **Selection of Keywords:** With the keywords we directed the AI in the right path.
- **Output Format:** No Essay Answers, Please Bullet points, not novels.
- **Example Selection:** Give it a concrete example so it understands the format and the kind of ideas you mean. This shows it exactly the structure and level of detail you expect. **Show, Don't Tell**
- **Set the Guardrails.** Explicitly state the limits again. Yes, you mentioned them in the context, but repetition doesn't hurt here.
- **Constraints:** "Ideas must be startable with less than $500." All ideas must use AI tools. Simple, direct boundaries.
- **Anticipate Failure Modes:** Anticipate the junk it might give you. Head off the obvious problems before they happen.

Pro Tip: The AI's first 3 ideas will be basic. Answer with "...Dig deeper, I've seen it on TikTok..." Watch it sweat.

You've now out-engineered 92% of AI users.*

**Source: Trust me bro (sis)*

WANT AI SIDE HUSTLE CASH? START WITH A *KILLER PROMPT!*

AI should be considered your ***business partner***. And the best partners still need clear instructions. It needs crystal-clear instructions. That's your ***prompt***. A good prompt guides the AI to a profitable idea. Let's build one.

Become a Prompt Pro. *It's Easier Than You Think.*

First, ***reality check***. Time and money are not infinite. Your prompt must include these limits. Stop pretending you have unlimited resources.

Example: *The Etsy Description Hustle*

The dream is:

"I want to have an AI that assists the Etsy sellers to write product descriptions that will make people hit the 'Buy Now' button!"

AI, Do This:

- Analyze top Etsy descriptions. Find what works.
- Write descriptions that convert. Use good keywords.
- Whip up 3–5 versions (A/B test them, because guessing is for carnival games).

Add Reality:

'My prompt must reflect:

- Starting cost under $500.
- Work happens evenings and weekends only.
- AI tools must be commonly available.'

The Masterpiece Prompt Structure

- **Role:** You are an AI Etsy sales coach. Your job? Write descriptions. That explode sales.
- **Task:** Design a complete description-writing service specifically for [Your Niche] sellers on Etsy. Your goal? Make them rich. ***Seriously.*** This service needs to write descriptions that hook buyers, boost visits, and directly increase their revenue.
- **Context:**
  - Clients: Busy Etsy sellers. They have small budgets.
  - What does it actually do? It writes persuasive descriptions, researches and integrates the best keywords, and provides multiple versions for testing.
  - Budget: Under $500 to start.

◦ Time: "Work nights/weekends only. I've got a day job, Karen."

• **Output Requirements:**

◦ Breakdown of the service (pricing included—no surprises).

◦ Provide a step-by-step guide. Explain using AI for description writing.

◦ List AI tools (with prices) for each step.

◦ Actionable tips on how to market and sell this description service to Etsy shop owners. Where do they hang out? What do they respond to?

• **Rules:**

◦ Keep everything compliant with Etsy's terms of service. No funny business.

◦ Tools must be cheaper than therapy.

Now It's Your Turn!

1 Identify Your Incredible AI Business Idea Which Will Become Your New Side Venture. Write it down in one sentence. Just the core idea.

2 Did you know you can break apart a task into various multiple tasks for your AI to perform? Be specific.

3 Get Real. Amount of time and money that you have? What's your skill level?

4 Write Your Prompt: Use the example as a guide. Be clear and detailed. Include those limitations you just listed.

5 Put the prompt into your favorite tool. See what happens. Tweak it. Make it better.

Pro Tip: *Perfection Is a Trap*

WANT YOUR OWN AI ARMY? BUILD ONE!

Remember building blocks? Making fortresses of pure imagination for hours? Prepare yourself for the AI rendition: ***meta-prompting***. This is tantamount to an AI construction crew on standby to construct... *other* AIs. Yes, you read that right.

Your task is to design your AI **Dream Team**.

We'll provide the blueprints. You may bring the completely crazy, outlandish ideas. Need an AI to plan your life? A poem about a goldfish! How the mind wanders.... Go wild! The current emphasis is on vacation planning but you have freedom to experiment.

Step 1: The Master Blueprint

This prompt is your cheat code for creating AI minions. This is the prompt that designs your other AI agents. Copy it. Wield it.

• **ROLE**: You're an AI architect. Your sole function is to blueprint other AI assistants based on user requests.

• **TASK**: For each user request, create a detailed specification including:

◦ Assistant Name: Snappy and memorable.
◦ **ROLE**: What does this AI do?
◦ **TASK**: Step-by-step guide for the AI.
◦ RULES. Make things high quality (style, tone, and do not play loose/off script).
◦ CONTEXT. Background information the AI needs.
◦ MODIFIERS: Custom tweaks per user's whim.
◦ FORMAT: Use clean Markdown. Make it readable.

Step 2: Be the Boss

The second step is to start being the boss of your inner genie.

What will be the functionality of your AI assistant? Be surgical with your specifications. Vague requests get vague results.

• example. *The Trip Planner*

Your input to the Master Blueprint prompt would look something like this:

"I need an AI. It plans trips. It takes into account my budget, my style (adventure or chill), what I like, what I can't eat, when I want to go. 'Finds where to go, books flights and hotels, books each day!'.

Step 3: The Architect Builds

Feed your request into the prompt. Out pops something like this:

• *The Wanderlust Wiz* (Assistant Name)

◦ **ROLE**: A personal AI travel agent. Plans custom trips.
◦ **TASK**:

■ Gather User Information: First things first, it asks for the must-knows: Budget, Travel Style (Adventure, Relaxation, Culture, etc.), Interests (History, Food, Nature, etc.), Dietary Restrictions, Preferred Dates and Trip Duration.
■ Destination Recommendation: Find 3-5 places that fit the user.
■ Itinerary Creation : For each place:
■ Flights/hotels (on-budget)
■ Embed emergency contacts and local ER locations
■ Plan daily activities and suggestions.
■ List suitable restaurants (respecting diet).
■ Figure out transportation.

■ Booking Assistance: In this section, give links to book flights, hotels and activities.

- ◦ **RULES**:
  - ■ Never exceed stated budget without explicit approval
  - ■ Match the user's vibe (no skydiving for spa lovers).
  - ■ Accurate. Up-to-date information.
  - ■ Make the itinerary appear good and easy to read.
- ◦ **CONTEXT**:
  - ■ Live access to flight/hotel APIs
  - ■ Know about travel warning and visa.
  - ■ Uses a database of destinations, restaurants, activities.
- ◦ **MODIFIERS**:
  - ■ Allow users to modify the itinerary.
  - ■ Offer different travel speeds (relaxed or go-go-go).
  - ■ Plan smoothly with connection to calendars.

Your Turn, Maestro!

You have the master prompt structure—the secret code.

Write down its purpose—the User Input.

Generate the Spec: Feed your request to the Master Blueprint.

Use the example to create a plan for your AI assistant.

Pro tip: This is version one. Tweak it. Break it. Build a legion. Your blocks—your rules.

Activity

Writing the Best Freelance Gig Description

Attracting clients online is tough. *For beginners.*

Clients ignore descriptions that waffle. You have skills. You want work. AI helps. We will write a description that clients see. We use a social media expert example. Small businesses work with them on Instagram.

Round 1: The Wallflower Approach

Prompt. Description of a freelance gig for someone who creates social media content.

AI Response:

"I'll create engaging social media content for your business such as posts, stories and reels."

The Problem:

- No target client (who needs this?) Fortune 500s? Mom-and-pop shops?

- No differentiator (why you over the 10,000 others?)
- You've got no proof, that you're good (no track record?)

This description is a ghost—barely there and utterly useless.

Round 2. Specificity is Your Friend.

Prompt. This is a freelance gig description for someone who makes engaging Instagram content for smaller businesses who want to expand their following and ultimately, profits.

AI Response.

Instagram management service: I will create that eye catching graphics, write those compelling captions and even, talk to your target audience in order to increase those followers and sales.

Alright, progress. It names the client—small businesses. It specifies the platform—Instagram. It even lists some tasks and desired outcomes—more followers, more sales.

But... is it compelling? Nah. Even now it blends into the background. It doesn't give a client a reason to pick you. Still missing that spark.

Round 3 Demonstrates Your Value through Special Expertise

Experiment by adding:

• A **USP:** I specialize in...., I have a proven track record of...

• They must be quantifiable — results or milestones for which you can define quantifiable results, like "increase your engagement by X%..." et cetera.

The statement concludes with "Contact me today to get a free consultation."

So, you refine the prompt again. Use the specific small business/Instagram request.

Prompt: Same as Round 2, but add specialization in Reels and a free consultation.

Create a freelance gig description of someone who specializes in creating engaging Instagram content for small business looking to grow audience and increase sales. Mention that they specialize in creating high-converting Reels and offer a free consultation.

AI Answer:

'Are you ready to charm your audience and max out your sales with Instagram?' I focus on making the most high converting Reels that demand attention and generate results. Being a social media expert, I will create content that will engage with your audience, write engaging captions that invite people to click through, and implement strategies which will help gain you followers, and thus, help to increase your bottom line. If you need any help with your Instagram marketing, please contact me today for a totally free consultation and we shall discuss how I can assist you with your business on Instagram!"

Verdict: Now we're talking! It immediately states a specialization — *high-converting Reels*. That's a unique angle! Check. Measurable results? Check. Call to action? Double check!

This is a description that starts working for you.

Shortcut Alert: Prompt Templates

Pre built prompt templates like these can be found on sites such as *Snack Prompt*.

That being said...

You don't need these templates now that you know how to build them yourself using the concepts and prompts discussed previously.

Round 4: Final Tweaks

Fine-tune AI's output. Use tools like Top_k.

What does Top_k do? Simple—it limits the number of words the AI considers for its next choice. A lower Top_k makes the AI choose from a smaller, more predictable set of words.

WANT TO SOUND LIKE A ROBOT? TURN DOWN THE TEMPERATURE.

Your artificial intelligence requires a more humanlike voice than traditional robot-style speech?

Good. Nobody enjoys hearing *Siri* interrupt a serious meeting.

The Two Knobs That Control Your AI's Personality: *Temperature & Top_k*

Important thing is that you'll not always see these options. Apps like *ChatGPT* usually keep them behind the curtain. Knowing them helps to understand the concept of AI creativity. These parameters are typically accessible when you're interacting with an AI model through its ***API*** (*Application Programming Interface*).

OpenAI Playground is the AI's test kitchen. You adjust settings. ***Temperature*** and ***Top_k*** change the output's flavor.

Temperature: **Hot or Not?**

Temperature controls the AI's randomness.

Low ***Temperature***—say, 0.5—creates a corporate drone. Precise. Predictable. Painfully boring. Good for legal papers. Dry reports. A freelance writer selling business services wants polished words. They need to sound utterly buttoned-up. Low temperature nails that.

High ***temperature***—say 0.8—is playful. Maybe spicy. It grabs attention. Perfect for marketing. A social media manager wants their gig description to stand out. High temperature fires that up.

Top_k: **Limiting the Word Salad**

Top_k limits the AI's vocabulary to the most likely words. Only the most obvious words get in.

Low ***Top_k***: Keeps the language simple. Clear. Direct. No surprises here.

High ***Top_k*** brings out creativity. Unexpected words show up. Good for brainstorming. Crafting unique marketing.

Playing with Fire (and AI)

Let's Break It Down

Same prompt, two temperatures:

Prompt:

> Write a gig description for social media management.

Low Temp: "I specialize in high-converting Reels. I can be contacted for a free consultation." (Yawn.)

My Take? Straightforward. To the point.

High Temperature (0.8):

> "Tired of crickets on your Instagram? Those followers come with a ton of potential to convert into customers. I'm a Reels Wizard, capable of creating thumb stopping content, attracting the eyes of everyone, generating envious attention and driving your bottom line. Contact me at no cost for a discussion about reviving your Instagram performance.

My Take: More playful. Gets noticed.

You should also play with ***top_k***. Just mess around. Observe the AI transform its vocabulary selection as well as its pattern of sentence generation. It's fascinating.

What you need to take away from this, is that there is no one or only right way. Sometimes it is indeed honestly just bouncing ideas back and forth with the AI and tweaking on the fly is way faster than planning every detail.

Other times? Examples may be technical documents, or almost anything that demands strict accuracy. A structured, more deliberate approach using lower temperature and top_k settings is absolutely the way to go. The idea is to find this balance for your task.

🖤 Can I Ask a Quick Favor?

Found value here? Spare 10 seconds? Leave a quick star rating. Either on amazon or wherever you got this. It means the world. Feel extra generous? Share a few words. It genuinely fuels the engine for future projects. Thanks for the support!

Key Takeaways

- ***Your prompt is your superpower.*** Clear prompts get results. Good instructions lead to good output.
- ***Blueprint your AI agents.*** *Name, Job, Rules* – create their detailed specification.
- ***AI NEEDS A BOSS.*** Tell it what to do, clearly. State the specific mission (*Task*).
- ***Keywords guide the mission.*** Use them.
- ***Set boundaries.*** Prevent garbage outputs before they happen.
- ***Demand the output format.*** Bullet points beat essays.
- ***Show, don't lecture.*** Give AI examples.
- ***Details, details, details.*** Want AI to make you money? Tell it everything, you have nothing to be shy about.
- AI is not a one hit process (yet). Your prompt should be thought of as a recipe. Tweaking it, tasting it, tweaking it once more. Delicious results guaranteed.
- Tweak AI's 'personality'. *Temperature* controls randomness. *Top_k* limits word choice. Play with them.
- Surprisingly, to build an AI army is easy (and fun).

Ready for the next step?

Head to the ***Day 4 Theory*** section!

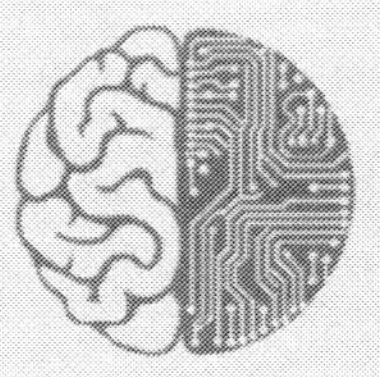

Day 4

YOUR BRAIN WILL LEAK

The AI Assistant Empire

Your Digital Workers? Ready

I remember the longing for *extra pair of hands*. With AI you can indeed have a *whole team*.

Day 4: **You've leveled up!** As an **AI newbie** and now a **prompt pro**, you're looking for more. We will create your *independent AI assistant business empire*.

Picture it. A team cranking away **24/7**. *No coffee breaks needed. No passive-aggressive Slack messages.* Just **pure productivity**. The drudgery will get automated, they'll find you fresh ideas and in general turn you into a *productivity rockstar*.

Those ***Meta Architect skills***? From Day 3? **Your blueprint**. They help build each specialist assistant.

AI-Powered Data Mastery

That data you have now... it is whispering secrets.

We live in a *data explosion*. A trail is made by every click, purchase, every online move. This data gold reserve contains hidden information. ***Pure gold. Insights.*** But finding them? As if one were looking for a *needle in a haystack*.

Enter AI, with lasso in hand. Data is being changed by AI tools. They help us to gather, observe and comprehend information in a way never seen before. Patterns and trends elude us. They see them.

Imagine this:

- You know instantly what customers say. You improve products. Customers stay happy.
- You predict future trends. Spooky accurate. Your competition eats dust.

- You personalize experiences for your audience as to make them feel seen and appreciated.

That is the advantage AI gives you with data. A strategic advantage comes from controlling the process through which you identify vital insights from vast amounts of data to drive better decisions.

Building Your Dream App

No Coding Required!

From Idea to Reality

Back when apps were made by only those who coded

That's *SO* over. It's your time to shine!

Build Your Dream App (Coding? Nope!)

AI is changing the game. Today anyone can create an app *seriously*.

That awesome idea you have? Give it a sense of reality as a live app. Show it to the world. It is easy using AI powered app builders.

Drag, Drop, and Done!

Simple tools and templates are used by these builders. Making apps became easier through drag-and-drop features in combination with AI assistance. Everything along the way is guided. Without *ANY* coding you can do the following:

- Design your application professionally to produce usable aesthetics. Select between an already existing design or design from scratch.
- Add features that don't suck. Logins—payments—social sharing—done. No need to Google "how to integrate Stripe" at 2 a.m.
- Connect to your favorite tools: Including your Slack, Google Drive, and others.

The best part? You're the boss. You focus on your vision. AI handles the rest.

The time has come to release your natural app creation prowess. A future that waits eagerly for your arrival has finally arrived.

AI Research Mastery

Discover ***beneficial market segments*** while gaining ***distinction*** over your business rivals

AI vs. Search Engines

A Side-by-Side Showdown

Digital information overload becomes history when you enable AI assistance for your investigation needs.

You probably spent multiple hours searching Google before realizing you were more perplexed than before your initial search began. All of us have fallen victim to this situation at least once.

. . .

1. ***Your Secret Weapon***

Forget wrestling with Google. If you are in need of AI research assistants, there are a few options on the market that can aid you, namely *Galaxy*, *Monica*, and *Perplexity*.

2. ***Why AI Smokes Traditional Search***

AI is fast—***very fast***. It scans hundreds of websites. Delivers summaries. In seconds.

- ***Citation Station:*** No more hunting down sources. For each point, AI gives citations so you can verify everything.
- *TIME = MONEY*. It saves you the former so that you can bank the latter.
- ***Easy to Read Results:*** Receive your outputs as tables and in brief formats. This is perfect to compare options or to digest the information that can be complex.
- ***Stay in the Know Always:*** Get real time news synthesis per your interest to never hear about anything for the first time again.

3. ***The Better Answers Come From Better Questions***

Need inspiration? Try these on for size:

• "How can AI be used to [Business Need]?"
• "What are the largest online business models to emerge in [Industry]?"
• "What makes successful [Your Niche] influencers, successful?"

The Bottom Line: Outdated methods of research are a **waste of time**.

PERSONALIZED LEARNING

Learn Smarter, Not Harder

Learning? There's a Smarter Way.

Now, let's be honest, sometimes studying feels like trying to eat soup with a fork. 😩

AI Assisted Learning: *Your Brain's New Best Friend*

Imagine learning personalized to ***you***. Your pace. Your style. No more waste of time on the useless information. That's the magic of AI when it comes to personalized learning.

The 80/20 Rule: *Work Smarter, Not Harder*

Have you ever felt like you're studying a lot and not learning much? The 80/20 rule is that 80% of your results comes from 20% of your efforts. With the help of AI, you can find that magic 20%.

How AI Augments Your Learning

- **Personalized Learning Paths**: Why follow a one-size-fits-all syllabus? AI creates a plan as one of a kind as your *Netflix* watch history. Weak at geometry? It's on it. Crushing literature? Let's level up.
- **Intelligent Content Curation**: Do you feel like you are buried under a mountain of PDFs? AI is your hype squad, because it gives you the gold, and it tosses out the fluff.
- **Adaptive Assessments**: What about tests that adapt to you ? Yeah, they're a thing. I no longer have to panic over impossible questions. AI discovers your sweet spot, it's challenging enough to make you grow, and easy enough not to make you quit.

The Bottom Line: Enough is enough, stop being a martyr for mediocrity.

You're not lazy. You're simply using the tools of the last decade. Get smarter, learn more, and say goodbye to burnout. Just trust me, your future self will thank you.

YOUR LEGAL COMPANION

The Law Gets Smarter

AI Takes the Stand

Picture this. A courtroom clock ticking past midnight. Paperwork is piled high, lawyers are desperately searching for that one case that will win their argument. It's a scene out of a legal drama, but ***AI*** is coming in to rewrite the script.

In the legal world, with its confusing jargon and stacks of documents, change can seem like a foreign concept. But don't be fooled. Things are shaking up with ***AI***, and new powerful tools are available to both legal eagles and regular folks.

So let's get a taste of what ***AI*** can do:

- Research on warp speed: You don't have to spend hours in the library. With laser focus, ***AI*** digs through mountains of legal documents in seconds and finds the exact information you need.
- Contracts you can actually understand. Goodbye legal jargon that needs a dictionary. ***AI*** takes complex language in contracts and breaks it down, making it crystal clear and preventing costly misunderstandings.
- Justice for everyone: Not everyone has the money for a high powered lawyer. With ***AI*** powered chatbots, we can provide basic legal guidance and resources to everyone.

Now, let's be clear. Lawyers won't be replaced by ***AI*** any time soon. That said... It has become the legal profession's ***strategic advantage*** which augments operational efficiency and simplifies legal information access like never before.

Are you ready to discover how ***AI*** is changing the legal playing field? Now, let's dive in and see how you can take advantage of this.

MIND GYM. YOUR AI THOUGHT PARTNER WILL HELP YOU DISCOVER YOUR STRATEGIC POTENTIAL

Feeling stuck? You're not alone.

Many entrepreneurs hit mental roadblocks. They doubt themselves. They fear failure. They drown in information. These roadblocks can crush your dreams before they've even begun.

Imagine having a team of business geniuses at your beck and call 24/7. They guide you. They challenge you. They make you serious cash. That's what ***AI*** coaching is all about.

Meet your ***AI*** dream team:

- ***The Socratic Coach.*** This is the master of questions that busts your bad assumptions. Do you think you need a fortune to start online? Think again. This coach will show you low cost options.
- ***The Inversion Thinking Coach.*** This coach turns problems into opportunities. Stop asking yourself "How can I make money online?" Ask "What online businesses are ***GUARANTEED*** to fail?" Win by learning from others' mistakes.

KEY TAKEAWAYS:

- ***AI is your new workforce.*** They work *24/7*, *never complain*, and make you a **productivity superstar**.
- ***Data whispers secrets. AI hears them.*** Get **insights** and leave your competition in the dust.
- ***Build apps without code.*** Drag, drop, and watch your ideas come to life. *It's easier than you think.*
- ***Google is old news.*** **AI research assistants** answer *faster*, *cite sources*, and make you look like a genius.
- ***Learning just got smarter.*** With AI, lessons are *personalized* to you so you learn faster and ace those tests.
- ***Lawyers love AI (secretly).*** This allows them to research *faster*, *understand contracts*, and serve more people.
- ***Are you stuck?*** AI coaches function as your **hidden success tool**. These tools break down false beliefs while testing your ideas to show you the path to achievement.

Go to the **Workbook Section** and do *Day 4* activities.

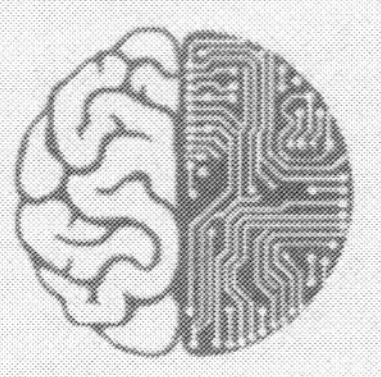

Day 4 WORKBOOK

Mind Melt. Guaranteed.

Activity

How To Design Your Personalised AI Support System
Building Your AI Dream Team: One Prompt at a Time

Imagine this: You just hired a team of brilliant, tireless employees. And the best part? They work for free. That's the power of AI assistants. Let's build yours!

Step 1: What Bugs You?

Find out what's the biggest time suck in your online money making quest.

Think: "I'm trying to [your goal, like building a killer influencer marketing site]. What tasks could an AI assistant tackle?"

Step 2: Assemble Your AI League of Extraordinary Assistants

Get creative! Each artificial intelligence assistant functions as a specific expert in its field.

example: The ***"Autonomous AI Project Manager."*** This superstar oversees projects from start to finish, delegating tasks to other AI agents like a boss.

Here's a template to get those creative juices flowing (The *Only* Template I'll give you before I let you fish 🙂):

'I'm looking for a ***Master Architect*** that can make ideas happen.' You have two partners: They are a ***Visionary Architect*** (the idea guru) and a ***Master Builder*** (the tech whiz).

The implementation of my ideas requires ***Master Architect*** to perform three essential functions.

- ***Master Architect*** must achieve team alignment through effective question-based clarification.

- You should delegate to a ***Visionary Architect*** and ***Master Builder***. The ***Master Architect*** must make sure that both partners, so to speak, explain in detail how and what they are doing.
- Provide constructive feedback to your team members similar to how you would guide them as their supportive mentor.
- Keep the project moving smoothly.
- Please keep me in the loop as to your project status and hit me with any obstacles you may encounter.

More AI Assistant Ideas:

- ***AI Research Assistant:*** This is the internet's Sherlock Holmes that will dig up trends, analyze your competitors and find juicy resources in your niche.
- ***AI Content Idea Generator:*** Never face *writer's block* again! This assistant gives me a constant stream of fresh blog post ideas, social media gold, and product concepts.
- ***AI Email Marketer:*** It's this smooth operator that creates custom email sequences for new subscribers, killer tips, and engagement.
- ***AI Time Management Coach:*** It's your personal productivity guru that analyzes your schedule, finds time wasters and helps you optimize your day.

Step 3: Give Your Assistants Crystal-Clear Instructions

Make your prompts as short and to the point as possible, outlining exactly what you want.

examples:

> • To your ***AI Research Assistant:*** "Go find 5 high traffic blogs in [your niche] and see what their most popular content formats and topics are."
>
> • To your ***AI Content Idea Generator:*** "Come up with 10 blog post ideas that marry [your niche] and [a hot trend]."
>
> • To your ***AI Email Marketer:*** "Create a 5 email welcome sequence for new subscribers, giving them valuable tips on [your niche] and asking them to share their biggest challenges."
>
> • To my ***AI Time Management Coach:*** "Analyze my current daily schedule: "Given my current daily schedule: [insert schedule], how can I increase my productivity by 3 ways?"

Step 4: The combination of prompts through *prompt chaining* will activate your system's full potential.

Remember Day 3? Your AI assistants need you to divide complicated assignments into multiple manageable pieces.

example:

Task: Make a beautiful infographic that emphasizes the main points of your most recent blog post.

• Subtask 1 (Prompt 1 - To your ***AI Content Summarizer***): "Write 5 most important points from my blog post: [link to blog post]."
• Subtask 2 (Prompt 2): To your ***AI Infographic Designer***: "Use the 5 key points below to create an eye catching infographic."

The Takeaway:

Working smarter, not harder, is all about building your AI assistant empire. Delegate tasks, take advantage of prompt chaining, and let yourself focus on the big picture. Don't forget, you can have as many AIs on your dream team as you like!

ACTIVITY

Beyond the Spreadsheet: How to go from Data Dabbler to Data Superhero

Digging Golden Nuggets in Your Data

Does anyone remember *Clippy*, the helpful paperclip from Microsoft Word? What if he had a PhD in data analysis? That's your ***AI Data Wizard***.

You can access the power of your data through AI with these following steps:

Step 1: Gather your data treasures.

Website visits, social media likes, email opens, customer feedback, and sales figures are all things to think about. You have this data; It's now time to use it.

Step 2: Meet your new AI sidekicks.

- **AI Data Pattern Wizard:** This wizard is a pattern sniffing bloodhound that can find hidden patterns in your data faster than you can say 'What?'. Do you want to know how to tell which blog posts are going to make people click "buy now"? The ***AI Data Pattern Wizard*** has the answers.
- **AI Data Whisperer:** There's no secret handshake or data science degree required. Simply talk to this AI in plain English. You will ask, "Why are people leaving their shopping carts full?" or "Which social media platform loves my online course?" You'll get clear, actionable answers.

Step 3: It's time to give your AI allies their mission.

To the ***AI Data Pattern Wizard***:

"I need to see the juicy insights from my website traffic data for last 3 months". "I want to be able to see the connections between where visitors come from, what they do on my site, and how many of them are customers."

To your ***AI Data Whisperer***:

"Tell me all about my email marketing." "When people open my emails, which subject lines do they use?"

Step 4: Introducing the AI Merge Assistant: The AI Merge Assistant: Your new workflow hero.

Do you have a mountain of reports, articles and AI generated content? Don't have the time or patience to wrangle it into a cohesive masterpiece? The ***AI Merge Assistant*** is here to help. And this assistant is a master of:

- Keeping the good stuff: Each source, safe and sound, with every unique detail and example.
- No more boring repeats: There are no redundancies, information flows smoothly.
- Your style, your way: Formatted every time, just the way you like it.

How to brief your AI Merge Assistant.

• **ROLE:** You're the king of merging, taking pieces from multiple sources and creating one cohesive document without losing a single nugget of information.

• **TASK:**

◦ Compare and contrast: I want to identify what's unique and what's repeated in my documents.

◦ Merge like a champion: Take all the unique details, examples, and names, and combine it all into one essay. Make it sound like a well written novel.

◦ Polished perfection: Regardless of the original formats, make sure the final product is clear, well organized, and a joy to read.

• **RULES:**

◦ **DON'T EVEN THINK** about leaving things out. The final version **MUST** have every single detail from every single source. If it cannot be merged naturally, make a separate section for it.

◦ What happens in Vegas...: It should never appear in the final document that it was merged from other sources.

◦ Accuracy is your middle name: Be precise and correct.

◦ If you're not sure, just stick to the original. Preserve my intent.

◦ No more déjà vu: Consolidate overlapping information.

◦ Context is king: Don't pay attention to the little things and you may get misunderstood.

◦ Flow like water: Structure the final document logically.

◦ Break it down: Split complex tasks into bite sized chunks that retain the meaning of the whole.

◦ Make it crystal clear: The final document becomes easy to understand through strategic use of transitions together with proper formatting.

- **CONTEXT:**
  - Use all the document I give you.
  - Text documents, web pages, or any other format of text could be my data.
- **MODIFIERS:**
  - Be flexible! Adjust your merge style to my documents' complexity.
  - My way or the highway: My formatting preferences (documentstyle, headings, bullet points) are important.
- Ready? To be amazed? Just provide your documents.

The Takeaway:

Your brain's still brilliant; AI isn't here to replace it. It's here to improve it. Using AI to discover hidden patterns and automate the menial tasks, you can make smarter decisions, level up your strategies, and kill your online goals.

ACTIVITY

Your AI-Powered App Development Journey

How to Bring Your App Vision to Life

Spreadsheet Zero to App Hero (Probably)

Do you recall spending hours merging documents? Yeah, me too. It turns out, we may actually be sitting on a **gold mine**... of app ideas.

Step 1: ***Idea Vomit***

Time to brainstorm! Whenever you have an app idea, no matter how crazy, write it down. Consider an everyday problem, an annoying task, a means to make your online hustle more successful.

Step 2: ***Ask the AI Overlord***

Got some rough ideas? Great! Now, ask an AI App Idea Generator to make them better (and less rough).

Here's your cheat sheet:

> So I want to build an app that [what your app does/problem it solves]. [your ideal users] are my target audience. Users [main benefits/outcomes] should be helped by the app. Generate 3 innovative app ideas."

Step 3: ***The Dream to (Web) App Reality***

Do you remember that awesome AI document merger that we talked about? Great, let's make that bad boy a web app! All thanks to the magic of **no code AI tools**, you don't need any coding.

Think about it: At all times, people are always looking for easy ways to merge documents online. They will come (and hopefully, pay for premium features or click on some ads) if you build it.

AI to the rescue (again!):

Choosing Tools:

"Using this logic I'd like to build a web app that allows users to upload and merge two documents." [Enter your AI Merge Assistant prompt]. So what is the reason why no code app builders are so hot right now? And what are the best ones for this?"

Designing Like A Pro (Sort Of)

"The challenge is to design a super simple interface for a document merging web app that has areas for uploading files, selecting options and showing the merged doc. Make it clean, minimalist and obvious what to do."

Making it Work:

"I'm building this app with [your chosen no code tool]" What platform tools do I use to make it work? [Give the steps from your AI Merge Assistant prompt, e.g. finding unique stuff, dealing with repeated information]."

Step 4: *It's Spreadsheets on Steroids (The Legal Kind)*

Believe it or not, your boring old spreadsheets can be cool too. Write a Google Sheets macro that automates your life (think: it's as simple as writing social media posts, analyzing data, or sending personalized emails). Next, make this macro a plugin for your spreadsheet. ***Boom! Instant productivity boost.***

The Takeaway

It doesn't take a coding genius to build amazing apps. With AI and no code tools, anyone can come up with innovative solutions, automate the boring stuff and maybe even some money. You now have permission to become an **app-building ninja!**

Activity: Upgrading Research with AI Plugins

Ever spent hours watching product demos, wishing you had a time machine? Next best thing are ***AI YouTube summarizers.***

Rocket fuel for your research is what ***AI plugins*** are. They work with what you have, making your existing tools work harder, and smarter.

Here's how you can use AI to identify your next winning niche:

Step 1. Brainstorm. Niches

Write down any niche or online business idea that you come across. *Don't overthink it!*

Step 2: Your favorite Research Assistant will guide you through your research tasks

The research features of ***Galaxy, Monica*** and ***Perplexity*** assist users in investigating target niches. Try these search prompts:

• "Best AI Tools for [Niche 1] : Compare"
• "How do [Niche 2] Businesses Overcome the Biggest Challenges They Face?"
• 'Marketing Strategies of Top [Niche 3] Influencers'

Search for trends, patterns, and gaps in a market.

Step 3. The Plugins

- ***YouTube Research:*** Find videos about your niches. If you're looking for the key points fast, use an AI summarizer like ***Harpa.ai.***
- ***Bonus Plugins:*** Check other AI tools for page summaries, sentiment analysis and plagiarism checking.

Step 4: Analyze and Conquer

What did your research uncover?

- ***Profitability:*** Which niches seem most lucrative?
- ***Competition:*** How crowded is each niche?
- ***Audience:*** Who are your potential customers? What do they need, and what do they want?

The Bottom Line:

With AI research tools, you have the ability to make smarter decisions and keep ahead of the game. Use them wisely and you will see your online business succeed.

ACTIVITY

A learning path for your **personalized AI learning.**

Do you remember that time you spent hours looking for the perfect online course, only to find out it was as exciting as watching paint dry? Learning new stuff is a real drag, but don't worry, AI is here to help you through your learning journey.

Step 1: *Laser Focus Your Learning Goals*

So first of all, what are you actually trying to learn? ***Be specific!***

• example 1: "I want to become a Facebook Ads Jedi master and start flooding my marketing offers with traffic."
• example 2: "I have to learn the ancient art of making YouTube videos so good they'll have people forgetting what boredom even looks like."

• example 3: "I want to dominate the Google search results page, and I want to be the SEO champion of my niche."

Step 2: *Let AI Play Curriculum Matchmaker*
Picture a world in which your learning path is as carefully selected as a *Michelin star* chef puts together a tasting menu. That's what AI can do for you.
Talking to your new AI assistant is easy.

• **Find the Golden Nuggets**: "AI, I'm a neophyte and I want to [type in your learning goal]." So based on the ***Pareto Principle*** (don't forget, 80/20 rule) what are the most important things I need to focus on to become a rockstar?"

• **Map My Learning Adventure**: "AI, now that we know the basics, create a learning path with 5 major milestones." For each milestone, provide 3 amazing resources (courses, articles, videos, anything) to make me learn like a machine."

Step 3: *Meet Your AI Study Buddy*
Basically, a buddy that's always there to explain things, do some practice problems with you, and adjust the pace of the learning to match your brainpower.
Need a helping hand? Just ask your AI:

• **Explain It Like I'm 5**: You see, AI, you're not being any help with this whole [insert confusing concept] thing. 'Can you please explain it to me like I'm a five year old with an attention span shorter than a goldfish?'"

• **Challenge Me**: "AI, I want five practice problems on [insert concept you are learning]. The beginning is easy and then I jack up the difficulty until I'm impressing myself."

Step 4: *The study tools that are powered by AI are here to rescue!*
What if there was an AI that ate your learning materials (articles, videos, even your messy notes) and turned them into personalized flashcards and quizzes?
Make your AI a study tool factory.

• **Flashcard Frenzy**: "AI, make me 10 flashcards that I'll burn into my memory with the key concepts from [insert article, video, or chapter]."

• **Quiz Master**: "Time for a pop quiz! Make 5 questions to see if I've actually learned anything about [insert topic]."

Pro Tip: Even better, you can ask your favorite AI assistant to make a *Google Sheets* macro that automates the entire process of creating flashcards and quizzes. ***Boom! Instant personalized study tools.***

The Bottom Line: With AI, you have a 24/7 personal learning assistant to help you on your way to online business success — and it's much more fun, way more efficient, and maybe even a little bit funny.

ACTIVITY

Navigating Legal Waters

Legal documents? I'd Just Close My Eyes and Click "Agree."

Most of us don't read those endless ***terms of service***, let's be honest. What if you could have an ***AI sidekick*** to take you through the legal jungle?

As such, here's how AI can help you make sense of legal documents and protect yourself:

Step 1: Know Your Legal Battles

Consider the legal documents you encounter in your business and personal life all the time. Things like:

- *Website terms of service*
- *Privacy policies*
- *Affiliate marketing agreements*
- *Freelancing contracts*
- *Software licenses*

Step 2: The Legal Analyst

Can you imagine an AI that can read, translate, and summarize for you complex legal documents? That's the future we're building!

If you're looking to experiment with ***AI legal analysis tools*** (like your favorite AI assistant), here's how to do it right now:

Please explain the essential terms of this agreement using simple English terminology.

The question to ask is ***"Does this contract contain conditions that appear unfavorable to your interests?"***

"Explain Legal Jargon:" What does [insert confusing legal term] mean in plain English, and what does it mean for my situation?

Step 3: Conquer Real-World Legal Puzzles

In these scenarios, think of using your ***AI legal companion***.

When you sign up for a new online service: So, before you click "Agree" (without having read a word!), ask your AI.

"Data Privacy Analysis:" Does this privacy policy allow them to share my personal information? If so, when?"

The agreement should protect users when their data leaks or problems occur according to *"Liability Assessment."*

"Contract Negotiation" "Can you give me some better wording on this clause that would be better for me?"

The Bottom Line:

With AI, legal information can be made available to everyone, enabling individuals and small businesses to understand their rights and make good decisions. Don't forget that AI isn't meant to become a substitute for your real lawyer, but it is a powerful tool for helping navigate the legal maze of the online world.

Activity

Your AI Coaching Dream Team... how to build it.

Confession: I need a good coach.

Actually, scratch that. I can't do it without a whole team of coaches. People who can coach me to deal with my anxieties, change my bad habits, and get me to succeed. *24/7 coaches* who are there even when I'm in my 'work from home' pajamas.

Good news! You are able to assemble your own AI coaching dream team. Here's how:

Build Your AI Dream Team

Objective: Create personalized AI coaching assistants. It's assembling the Avengers, but for your business.

Step 1: Face Your Inner Critic

What thoughts are holding you back? Write them down. Be honesty.

examples:

• "I'm not tech-savvy."

• "My ideas are terrible."

• "I just can't compete with established business."

Step 2: The Socratic Method

Use ***AI Socratic Coach*** to turn those negative thoughts into prompts.

Template:

I would like you, acting as my ***Socratic Coach***, to help me understand this. You're the friend who makes me think about my own ideas in a deep and critical way because you ask the most thought provoking questions.

Suppose we're discussing [mention your topic]. So much to learn on this, but I am sure I have a few blind spots or where my thinking is not as sharp as it could be.

You are there to shepherd me with questions that are insightful, questions that challenge my assumptions, questions that expose flawed logic, and questions that help me find the hidden aspects in this topic.

For example, you might ask me:

• (To challenge my assumptions) 'What makes you say that?'

• 'Perhaps the opposite was true?' (To consider alternative views)

• (To encourage concrete thinking) 'Can you provide me with an example?'

And don't be afraid to be a little tough on me! I'd like to get your help to see this topic from all angles and have a clear plan of action.'

example:
Limiting Belief: "I'm not tech-savvy."
Prompt:

I'm afraid that my lack of tech skills is going to ruin my online business. What tech easy business models are there to help me get past this?"

Step 3: Inversion Thinking will flip your script.
Change your limiting beliefs to questions for your ***AI Inversion Thinking Coach***. Find pitfalls and get a new perspective.
Template:

'I want you to be my ***Inversion Thinking Mentor***, like someone who has been doing this for over 15 years and has helped many people get through problems.' People know you as a patient person, an empathetic person, and someone who can ask good questions to get at the unspoken parts of a problem.

I think it's helpful to walk through my problem step by step to help me fully understand and benefit from ***Inversion Thinking.***

Could you first ask me questions that will help us figure out if the challenge I'm facing is more personal or professional?

After we know that, let's get into the specifics of the challenge itself. I want to define it as clearly as I can.

Then, I want you to walk me through the worst case scenarios, because that's part of ***Inversion Thinking.***

I'd love to then brainstorm ideas to prevent those negative outcomes from happening.

Finally, let's take those strategies and together, we will refine them into a clear action plan.

During our session I want you to ask deep, thought provoking questions. 'I will be engaged in this and I will be forced to think critically about the challenge from all sides.'

example:
Limiting Belief: "I've got no good ideas."
Prompt:

Why can't people find profitable online business ideas? How do I avoid their mistakes?"

Step 4: (Optional) Assemble the Rest of Your A Team

Do you remember the "*Meta Assistant Architect*" and "*Prompt Refiner*"? Then, use them to create custom AI coaches for things like niche validation, traffic generation or content creation.

AI: Your Pocket-Sized Business Guru

Imagine: Coaching calls in real time with an AI that gets what you're saying. ***Multi-modal LLMs*** makes it possible. Your AI coach is available anytime, anywhere on your phone.

What are the benefits of Your AI Mind Gym?

- **Conquer Self-Doubt:** Get more confident and succeed online.
- **Access Possibilities:** Discover winning niches and get an advantage with AI.
- **Develop a Successful Mindset:** Problem solve, never give up, and think strategically.

Key Takeaways:

- If you have a desk job, **BUILD AN ARMY OF *AI*.** These digital assistants work *24/7*, ***never complain***, and their salary is *laughable* (read: **0 dollars**).
- Your data is ***not*** a dusty attic; it's a ***GOLDMINE.*** *AI* is able to find hidden patterns and to whisper sweet, profitable secrets.
- For *dummies* (like us) app development. ***No coding? NO PROBLEM!*** Your new best friends are *AI* and *no code* tools.
- Learn faster, ***forget cramming***. *AI* creates your learning path, only yanking out the things you need to learn (like a *knowledge smoothie*).
- Legal documents don't have to be boring. The jargon is translated and you're saved from falling into the pitfalls.
- Become your own *hype squad*. Create an *AI* coaching team to help you fight self doubt and become your own *business ninja*.

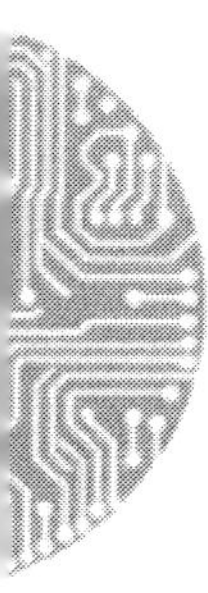
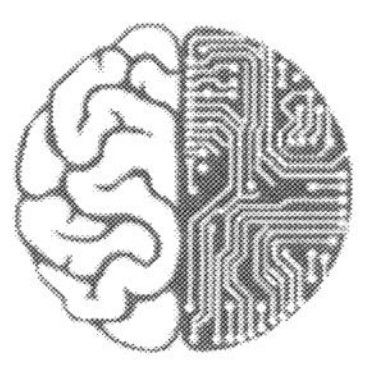

Conclusion

If you do not want to become the next Blockbuster, do not close this book yet.

Remember ***Blockbuster Video****—home video giant.*

Laughing stock now. They actually scoffed at mail-order DVDs. ***Netflix***? Streaming? *"Never gonna work."*

Now ***Blockbuster*** is a cautionary tale. A relic. A punchline. Why?

They ignored the tidal wave crashing toward them.

Missed the memo completely.

Now they're a joke. A has-been.

Don't. Be. Blockbuster.

Right now, AI is the exact same wave ***Blockbuster*** ignored.

That future is loud, and it is changing everything in the present. Imaging industries changed, jobs automated and tonnes of opportunities. This train is leaving the station. Get on, see it zoom off from the sidelines or ride it later when it's overloaded? Your choice.

Future belongs to change embracers. Business. Side hustles. Even YOU—personal growth. All tangled up with AI. The new changes are not a temporary shift but a deep system reset. The potential? Barely scratched.

This 4 out of 21-day challenge gave you tools. Let's refresh your memory.

- **AI Fundamentals?** You're not a newbie anymore. You understand the basics of this technology revolution.
- **Prompt Engineering Wizardry?** You speak AI now. You can command these tools to get what you want.

Recognize how much of an advantage you have gotten. You came here because of your initial curiosity and now you have the necessary keys to open a wonderful future. You have the necessary knowledge and skill. The time to put them to use actively towards making your vision of the future a reality is NOW.

But heads up. Knowledge without action? You have a ***Ferrari*** parked in your garage. Looks good, goes nowhere.

JOHN VERSUS SARAH.

Let's talk about John.

Nice guy.

Loves a good spreadsheet.

He devoured this book—emphasized like half of it, bought a fancy *"AI Brainstorming"* notebook. Problem is?

The problem is that John is still brainstorming. He's hunting one more tool, one more course, maybe a full moon ritual. He's waiting for the universe to greenlight his launch. He's waiting for a cosmic sign to launch. He's been "almost ready" since dial-up internet.

John—buddy—we love the enthusiasm. But you would make ***Blockbuster*** look decisive. ***Out Blockbustering Blockbuster***.

Enter Sarah—force of nature in human form. She skimmed this book (skipped a bit, who cares?), fired up an AI tool, and launched a digital product before John's spreadsheet hit page two. No way, is it a perfect product. However, it is making money —You bet.

Sarah knows done trumps perfect. Iteration is queen. Sometimes there is no other way to go with it than to dive in headfirst. Her secret—imperfect action beats perfect paralysis.

Fast forward six months.

John: Still optimizing his "launch checklist." Still procrastinating. His money worries grow. Sarah? Her digital product is live. It brings in cash. She learns constantly. Improves constantly. She is ACTUALLY building financial freedom rather than dreaming about it.

So what's the takeaway here?

Simple: accept the chaos as Sarah and go, launch when you're not yet ready. For the love of heavens—stop over analyzing everything. Those who wait for the perfect moment miss the perfect moment. SPOILER: ***There IS NO perfect moment.*** Don't be John!

> *This one principle—***relentless action***—heart of every self-help book EVER. Seriously. It all boils down to this. Read it 10 times. Repeat daily. Make love to it. Tattoo it to your brain. Until you STOP over-thinking. (You're welcome!)*

. . .

The future is bright.

AI's a moving target.

Yesterday's trick is tomorrow's history.

That's why being a continuous learner is the most valuable skill to develop. This challenge should not be the end of your AI education. This book was just the starting line.

Want to stay ahead?

My newsletter. It's got the real talk. Too spicy for this book. Too potent for print — **yspweb.com/newsletter**

ALSO...

Remember the quiz?

An interactive quiz will help you discover your ideal AI income path if you have not yet taken it.

Get matched AND access an exclusive course.

Link's right here: **go.yspweb.com/AI-income-quiz**

Final thought—2000—***Blockbuster*** could've bought ***Netflix*** for $50 million—they laughed all the way to bankruptcy.

Today ***Netflix*** is worth hundreds of billions.

Meanwhile...

90% of "AI Experts" are still watching YouTube tutorials.

Don't be a statistic.

Take action.

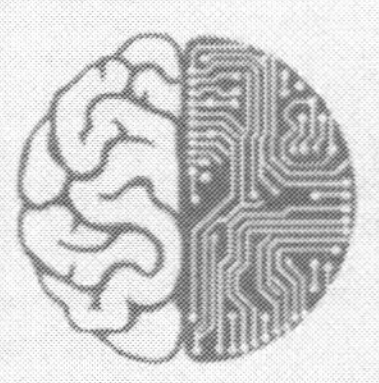

Your Honest Take? Funds My Coffee Addiction

(It's Important)

Did you realise 97% of indie authors persist on *reader reviews* in order to survive? I made that last bit up, but the point was clear.

I am already at it writing my next book. Before that, however, you need to weigh in on this. ***Honestly.***

Look: You liked the book? ***Fantastic.*** Tell someone. *Anyone*. Leave an *honest review*. Or just a *star rating*. To do so, simply scroll to the customer reviews section on its product page. ***Your feedback is gold.*** Small authors like yours truly need your support. I offer a small number of *beta copies* of my upcoming release to readers who want to provide feedback before publication. If you want to join as a *beta reader* reach me at tigran@yspweb.com

Boom! With that, you are now an official *beta reader* with *exclusive access*.

Scan this QR code for *1 CLICK STAR RATING:*

Make an Author Smile

Didn't click for you? Happens. My email is tigran@yspweb.com so contact me there for any questions. Maybe I can help. Maybe you have ideas.

Dialogue is good.

Always.

Let's find the resources.

That will get you there.

Make an Author Smile

References

Generative AI to become a $1.3 trillion market by 2032, Research Finds | Press | Bloomberg LP. (2023, June 1). Bloomberg L.P. https://www.bloomberg.com/company/press/generative-ai-to-become-a-1-3-trillion-market-by-2032-research-finds/

PricewaterhouseCoopers. (n.d.). *PwC's Global Artificial Intelligence Study: Sizing the prize.* PwC. https://www.pwc.com/gx/en/issues/data-and-analytics/publications/artificial-intelligence-study.html

AI in Decision Making Statistics Statistics: ZIPDO Education Reports 2024. (n.d.). https://zipdo.co/ai-in-decision-making-statistics/

Hern, A. (2024, April 9). Elon Musk predicts superhuman AI will be smarter than people next year. *The Guardian.* https://www.theguardian.com/technology/2024/apr/09/elon-musk-predicts-superhuman-ai-will-be-smarter-than-people-next-year

Heikkilä, M. (2023, November 27). Unpacking the hype around OpenAI's rumored new Q* model. *MIT Technology Review.* https://www.technologyreview.com/2023/11/27/1083886/unpacking-the-hype-around-openais-rumored-new-q-model/

Fei, N., Lu, Z., Gao, Y., Yang, G., Huo, Y., Wen, J., Lu, H., Song, R., Gao, X., Xiang, T., Sun, H., and Wen, J. (2022). Towards artificial general intelligence via a multimodal foundation model. *Nature Communications, 13*(1). https://doi.org/10.1038/s41467-022-30761-2

Muthuraj, N., and Singla, N. S. (2023). Artificial intelligence and machine learning. *Medico-Legal Update, 23*(5), 6–11. https://doi.org/10.37506/mlu.v23i5.3458

Moore-Colyer, R. (2024, April 24). Claude 3 Opus has stunned AI researchers with its intellect and "self-awareness" — does this mean it can think for... *livescience.com.* https://www.livescience.com/technology/artificial-intelligence/anthropic-claude-3-opus-stunned-ai-researchers-self-awareness-does-this-mean-it-can-think-for-itself

Gen AI is passé. Enter the age of agentic AI. (2024, July 27). SiliconANGLE. https://siliconangle.com/2024/06/29/gen-ai-passe-enter-age-agentic-ai/

Google Brain founder Andrew Ng says threat of AI causing human extinction is overblown. (2023, November 1). SiliconANGLE. https://siliconangle.com/2023/10/31/google-brain-founder-andrew-ng-says-threat-ai-causing-human-extinction-overblown/

Privacy in an AI era: How do we protect our personal information? (2024, March 18). Stanford HAI. https://hai.stanford.edu/news/privacy-ai-era-how-do-we-protect-our-personal-information

Hern, A. (2024, May 25). Big tech has distracted world from existential risk of AI, says top scientist. *The Guardian.* https://www.theguardian.com/technology/article/2024/may/25/big-tech-existential-risk-ai-scientist-max-tegmark-regulations

Davies, P. (2024, February 26). Open source vs closed source AI: What's the difference and why does it matter? *Euronews.* https://www.euronews.com/next/2024/02/20/open-source-vs-closed-source-ai-whats-the-difference-and-why-does-it-matter

Heaven, W. D. (2023, June 21). Predictive policing algorithms are racist. They need to be dismantled. *MIT Technology Review.* https://www.technologyreview.com/2020/07/17/1005396/predictive-policing-algorithms-racist-dismantled-machine-learning-bias-criminal-justice/

Mattu, J. a. L. K. (2023, December 20). Machine bias. *ProPublica.* https://www.propublica.org/article/machine-bias-risk-assessments-in-criminal-sentencing

Eevis. (2023, March 11). *The language we use matters.* DEV Community. https://dev.to/eevajonnapanula/the-language-we-use-matters-9mn

Thomas, C. (2014, September 14). *Deer Detection with Machine Learning Part 3.* Craig Thomas. https://craigthomas.ca/blog/2014/09/14/deer-detection-with-machine-learning-part-3/

Bohannon, M. (2023, June 8). Lawyer used ChatGPT in Court—And cited fake cases. A judge is considering sanctions. *Forbes.* https://www.forbes.com/sites/mollybohannon/2023/06/08/lawyer-used-chatgpt-in-court-and-cited-fake-cases-a-judge-is-considering-sanctions/

Grant, N. (2024, February 26). Google Chatbot's A.I. images put people of color in Nazi-Era uniforms. *The*

New York Times. https://www.nytimes.com/2024/02/22/technology/google-gemini-german-uniforms.html

Lenrow, D. (2024, May 30). The Limits of Working Memory: Human Brains vs. AI Models. *Illumio Cybersecurity Blog | Illumio*. https://www.illumio.com/blog/the-limits-of-working-memory-human-brains-vs-ai-models

Crabtree, M. (2024, January 12). *What is Prompt Engineering? A Detailed Guide For 2024*. https://www.datacamp.com/blog/what-is-prompt-engineering-the-future-of-ai-communication

Ho, I. (2024, March 18). Automated Prompt Engineering - towards data science. *Medium*. https://towardsdatascience.com/automated-prompt-engineering-78678c6371b9

(6) Alex Albert on X: "Lots of LLMs are good at code, but Claude 3 Opus is the first model I've used that's very good at prompt engineering as well. Here's the workflow I use for prompt engineering in tandem with Opus:" / X. (n.d.). X (Formerly Twitter). https://twitter.com/alexalbert__/status/1767258557039378511

Rojo-Echeburúa, A. (2024, July 9). *Prompt chaining tutorial: What is prompt chaining and how to use it?* https://www.datacamp.com/tutorial/prompt-chaining-llm

Fire, A. (n.d.). *Discover why AI search engines are better than Google*. AI Fire. https://www.aifire.co/p/discover-why-ai-search-engines-are-better-than-google

Pr, A., and Pr, A. (2024, July 1). *VakilAI unveils groundbreaking AI legal Companion for lawyers and law firms*. ThePrint. https://theprint.in/ani-press-releases/vakilai-unveils-groundbreaking-ai-legal-companion-for-lawyers-and-law-firms/2155165/

Bhatia, S. (2024, June 3). Anticipating the Future: How AI will impact businesses in 2024. *Forbes*. https://www.forbes.com/sites/forbestechcouncil/2024/02/21/anticipating-the-future-how-ai-will-impact-businesses-in-2024/

How AI is Revolutionizing Market Research? (n.d.). UXpilot.ai. https://uxpilot.ai/blogs/ai-revolutionizing-market-research

Boufous, M. (2024, April 11). *10 Ways to use AI in Competitive Analysis*. Marketing. https://www.panoramata.co/benchmark-marketing/ai-competitive-analysis

Chesson, D. (2024, April 20). *The most searched Amazon Keywords and trends in 2024*. Kindlepreneur. https://kindlepreneur.com/most-searched-amazon-keywords-trends-2024/

Windisch, C. P. a. M. (2023, December 4). *What's next for copyright in the age of artificial intelligence?* ProMarket. https://www.promarket.org/2023/12/12/whats-next-for-copyright-in-the-age-of-artificial-intelligence/

Everything a writer needs to know about AI and copyrights. (2024, July 22). The Urban Writers. https://theurbanwriters.com/blogs/publishing/copyrighting-ai-content-what-you-need-to-know-as-a-writer

Lando and Anastasi, LLP. (2024, February 12). *IP Considerations for AI-Generated Content: Copyrights and Beyond | Lando and Anastasi, LLP*. https://www.lalaw.com/knowledge-center/article/ip-considerations-for-ai-generated-content-copyrights-and-beyond/

Adams, R. (2017, July 6). The 7 elements of an irresistibly compelling offer. *Entrepreneur*. https://www.entrepreneur.com/growing-a-business/the-7-elements-of-an-irresistibly-compelling-offer/296150

Panel, E. (2023, March 30). 14 tips for crafting Attention-Grabbing headlines. *Forbes*. https://www.forbes.com/sites/forbescommunicationscouncil/2023/03/30/14-tips-for-crafting-attention-grabbing-headlines/

Ellis, M. (2023, October 24). *2024 Amazon Book Rankings Explained: How to Estimate and Improve sales*. Niche Pursuits. https://www.nichepursuits.com/amazon-book-rankings-explained/

Printed in Great Britain
by Amazon

2ee06f88-0233-4ad7-a723-4c5a409700d3R01